Gene Vincent

There's One In Every Town

Also by Mick Farren, published by The Do-Not Press

The DNA Cowboys Trilogy
'The Quest of the DNA Cowboys' – 'Synaptic Manhunt'
'The Neural Atrocity'

GENE VINCENT

There's One In Every Town

Mick Farren

First Published in Great Britain in 2004 by
The Do-Not Press Limited
16 The Woodlands
London SE13 6TY
www.thedonotpress.com
email: gene@thedonotpress.com

ISBN 1 904 316 37 9

British Library Cataloguing in Publication Data. A catalogue record for this book is available from the British
Library.

1 3 5 7 9 10 8 6 4 2

Printed and bound in Great Britain

Contents

DEDICATION

For Joe Strummer, Joey Ramone, and the countless other singers who clung to a mike-stand as though their lives depended on it.

Skinny white sailor
The chances were slender, the beauties were
brief
May I mourn your decline with some
Thunderbird wine
And a black handkerchief
I miss your sad Virginia whisper
I miss the voice that called my heart
Sweet Gene Vincent
Young and old and gone
Who, who slapped John?
White face
Black shirt
White socks
Black shoes
Black hair
White Strat
Bled white
Died black
Sweet Gene Vincent

Ian Dury, *Sweet Gene Vincent*

Chapter One

THE CROWD FELT like it was ninety percent men and ten percent women, with the air of a young-male tribal ritual. An edge of violence was in the air. The sense of impending mayhem was the same as The Who would conjure a few fast years later, and The Clash would recreate in a decade and a half, but the Clash preached to punks, and The Who played to erupting mods. In the Brighton, Essoldo in 1961 there were no mods. The only mods of the time called themselves modernists, wore mascara and listened to Miles Davis, and were confined to the West End of London. The teenage, seaside riots were on down the timeline, just like The Who and The Clash. There and then, we were all rockers under the skin. We had even sat in the Essoldo, or one of the other holiday resort picture palaces, and watched all those Hollywood movies that had shaped a UK style; Steve McQueen and James Coburn in *The Magnificent Seven*, James Dean in *Rebel Without A Cause*, Paul Newman in *Left Handed Gun*, Robert Mitchum in *Night Of The Hunter*, and Richard Widmark as the sniggering-psychotic Tommy Udo in *Kiss of Death*. Marlon Brando and the late-great Lee Marvin in *The Wild One* had been banned in the UK, although a few in the crowd might have seen it at a members-only flea-pit called the Paris Cinema Club, where it was occasionally run between uncut Brigitte Bardot movies and Swedish nudie epics. We'd all seen the stills of Brando, though, and the style was still the vogue, and, if the interior of the Essoldo that night wasn't wall-to-wall, 59 Club leather jackets, such was certainly the illusion.

Drapes and the new Italian bum-freezers must have figured in the crowd, yeah, and probably some windbreakers and sensible sports jackets, but we didn't want to think that everything wasn't perfect, or that many of us simply couldn't afford to dress like an American pan-head Harley Davidson outlaw of six or seven years earlier. We had come to witness the great Gene Vincent, and were determined that all should be perfect, even if it required a certain suspension of disbelief.

We didn't have Elvis to preside over these communal rights of passage, but we had all turned out for what had to be the next best thing. For the night, Gene was to be the eye of our hurricane, and in some respects, for the time and the demographic, Gene Vincent was actually more important than Elvis Presley. Gene Vincent, you see, was ours. He was obtainable. His magic was within reach, and his role as rock 'n' roll magician was one to which we might just aspire. No one in their right mind could seriously aspire to be Elvis. The only exception was The Beatles, and, even then it took four of them to do what he did. With cheap guitars and a drummer who could borrow a van, we might, at the very fullest stretch of imaginations, dream of being Gene. Also Gene hadn't compromised. Unlike Elvis, Gene, crazy and underage, had enlisted in the navy, and had his military service behind him when fame and fortune came knocking. He wasn't drafted at the peak of his wildness. And mercifully wasn't in jail like Chuck Berry, hadn't lost his nerve and found Jesus like Little Richard. He was, however, about to go on the run. In the USA, debts, unpaid taxes, a shut-out from TV where, by the machinations of Dick Clarke, pretty boys called Bobby ruled the top forty, meant Gene and the other first-generation, primal rockers faced a rapidly dwindling audience. To our eternal good luck, Gene fled to Europe, and America's loss was our gain.

My memory is of a black-clad antihero in a white follow-spot, like the climax of a prison break turned bad. Top of the world, ma! Gene was not alone on the stage – far from it – he had all seven pieces of Sounds

Incorporated at his back, the best band that
money could buy in the UK in 1961, but he
still managed to generate a wrenching sense
of alienation, isolated in a personal
purgatory, dangerous and vulnerable, for all
the world like a man in the grip of some
darkly distorting religious experience. The
contorted figure in the black leather suit
stood with one leg forward, knee bent, and
the other, held rigid in a steel brace and
thrust awkwardly out behind him. The stance
was unnatural, you could maybe call it
unholy. His body seemed twisted, almost
tortured. At peaks in the act his whole frame
would vibrate as he clutched the microphone
stand with his gloved hands, desperately, as
though it was all that prevented him from
being born away by the rage and passion of
the moment. His corpse pale face was
framed, Dracula style, by the upturned collar
of his leather jacket, and a sweat soaked
bunch of grapes had collapsed on his
forehead. He had this trick of raising his eyes
to an imaginary point, high in the
auditorium, higher even that the cheap seats

in the upper balcony, as though he was staring into some unknown, Stephen King hell, at hovering, circling, malevolent angels, invisible to the rest of us.

For a man with a ruined leg, he was agile. At peaks of intensity, he would swing his damaged leg over the mike stand as the mob bayed its approval. During a solo that was crucial to the dynamic, he would mount flat top of the grand piano shouting un-miked, unheard words to guitars and horns as though he was Kirk Douglas leading his men over the top in *Paths of Glory* or Custer refusing to admit defeat. His power was that he gave the performance every last piece of himself. He took all the risks, chancing, it seemed, his own critical safety and survival, and courting either flame-out or burn-out. Six or seven years later, after rock 'n' roll went to college, Jim Morrison would attempt to articulate the tension of this theatrical craziness in terms of a return to Dionysian demonic shamanism. Gene, on the other hand, had no fancy learning, and behaved as though he had happened upon this fountain head of primal, Reichian energy, with no more clue than Jed Clampett when he struck oil and moved to Beverly Hills. Between songs Gene behaved with reticence, bemused, almost a deer in the headlights when confronted with the dark, angry-young-man magic he had raised with his invocation of 'Who Slapped John'. He hardly spoke or acknowledged the crowd, maybe unsure if he was the bull or the matador in this oh-so primitive drama, or perhaps too locked in to the business at hand to raise even Elvis Presley's bantering self-depreciation. For Gene it was a tentative, rote introduction. 'Got a little song here we'd like to play for you now. Goes like this.' A spread chord to give the man the note. 'Wwwwellll... '

And we'd all be off on the thrill ride again.

Back in those days, we South Coast kids who were too young to drive got around on Southern Region commuter trains that mercifully came without connecting corridors. These were local stopping trains serving

stations with passing names like Lancing,
East Worthing, Fishersgate Halt, Angmering,
that came at less than five minute intervals.
The constant threat of interruption thwarted
any prolonged pornographic imaginings of
unscrewing the compartment light bulbs and
totally turning the last train going west out of
Brighton into a rolling teenage bacchanalia,
but we did the best we could. On that train
back home, my hands were all over my date's
body and hers were all over mine. This, on
its own, was fortuitous but not unusual.
Some heavyweight groping on the train
home, with inhibitions lost to vodka and 7UP
were a suburban ritual, but I swear, this time
it was somehow different. The depth of need
was deeper and the woman rose to meet me,
equally hungry and angry, abandoning the
game of token, reputation-saving resistance.
I've already mentioned that the proportion of
women at a Gene Vincent show was
markedly low. The girls in the beehives,
puffed-out skirts and white stilettos thronged
auditoriums like the Essoldo for Cliff Richard
and Shadows; they turned out and screamed

for Adam Faith, and Billy Fury, backed by the Blue Flames, with Georgie Fame looking so cute on keyboards. On the other side of the side of the coin, however, the women how did show up for Gene or Jerry Lee Lewis had a tough and unique class, and took no fashion tips from Helen Shapiro.

The women who yelled for Gene and liked it could be factory workers, faux-hard diamonds before their time, or renegade convent girls already in full, if guilt-wracked, revolt against the celibate power of the nuns, but they all pretended to a gun moll style, if tempered with a certain skittish nervousness that they were walking a road that, by the reactionary morals and narrow proprieties of the time led straight to societal hell. In the future, they would take the pills, smoke the dope, drop the acid, some would sign on as bunnies at the Playboy club, others would become independent single mothers, groupies, singer-songwriters, or activists in the women's movement, but all that was years in the future. In the meantime, the wore their blue jeans skintight, tilted their hips, snapped their gum, sucked on a Consulate menthol cigarette, and cultivated a smart and cynical mouth. If nothing else, it was an attitude that positioned them well for all the upheavals and sexual insurrections to come.

What this woman and I were feeling on the train that night was more than just some proscribed foreplay gratification. Again the only words were primal or primitive. We needed to scream and howl, but we had yet to learn the knack of doing it. Instead, we clung to each other as if some violent merging was possible, urgent and desperate, with no alternatives, and damned if we wanted any. We had just been part of a dark congregation of post-fifties teen-lust, backed by the loudest electric guitars we had so far heard in our young lives. We had passed childhood's end but would kick and scream bloody murder before we'd allow ourselves to be forced into what was currently being promoted as maturity. We had, quite literally, been turned around, shown a direction that ran in complete opposition to the path the system had planned. We knew absolutely nothing of what was to come or what we could do, except that there had to be some yet unformed other way, a left hand path, without chart or map, but that offered a wild and dangerous hope that we could find the blind, bold courage we'd need stumble down it.

Such was the effect of a Gene, all those years ago. I firmly believed that rock 'n' roll harboured a solid, if unshaped core of insurrection, long before it could even form or spell the word.

Well, Carl Perkins was down South... we were all down South, actually. Carl Perkins, me, Elvis Presley; Bill Haley was up north. Haley was into saxophones and horns and things like that. When it all started out, they called it rockabilly. Perkins started first. Perkins was on his way to do the Ed Sullivan Show *when he hit a tractor and wrecked his back. So they said to themselves: who can we get to take his place? Well, they said that there was this boy called Elvis Presley and there's one called Gene Vincent. But I was in*

the hospital at that time and Presley did it.
On the Ed Sullivan Show.
            Gene Vincent, 1970

The kindest word is confusing. Gene Vincent's life, as currently recorded, is filled with conflicts, contradictions, and leaves much to be desired in the realm of hard facts. A drunken pillhead tends to be more concerned with legend than accuracy, and makes up the stories as he goes along. Add lawyers, process servers, ex-wives, ex-managers, and tax-collectors on two sides of the Atlantic, and a firewall of deliberate smokescreens comes into play, obscuring the names and dates. This seems to have been the way with Gene. Even his exact birth date is disputed. The popular version is that he was born Vincent Eugene Craddock, in the US Navy shipyard town of Norfolk, Virginia, on February 11th, 1935, just 34 days after Gladys Presley's surviving twin first saw daylight. His parents were Mary Louise Cooper and Ezekiah Jackson Craddock, farm folk, by all accounts, from North Carolina, who moved the short distance across the State Line to Norfolk. His childhood appears unremarkable except that he 'liked music and girls'. His sister Evelyn is quoted delivering a standard cliché of Norman Rockwell rock star origins, that has both Elvis and Jerry Lee Lewis peeking in to the honky-tonk, hearing the blues on the front porch, and thus being inculcated with the music of the devil. 'A black man lived down the street and he'd come to the store, an old country store, and we had chairs out there and he sang while Gene played.'

About the only real indication of the real nature of Gene's early years was that he couldn't even wait until his eighteenth birthday to run off and join the Navy, but, in this, he was little different to a whole host of Norfolk boys without skills, future, or even a high school diploma. As a matter of record, Gene Craddock formerly enlisted in the US Navy on February 19th, 1952. 'Cry' by Johnny Ray, and Hank Williams' 'Cold, Cold Heart' were both in the top forty, and the Korean War had entered its third year of hostilities. His sister Evelyn remembers Gene having an obsession with war movies and wanting to be shipped to Korea while the fighting was still there for the experiencing. The Navy, on the other hand, had different plans, and, after basic training, he was assigned to the tanker USS Chuckawan as a deck hand, and he sailed on a tour of the Mediterranean. He seemed to have a reasonable enough time in his first three year hitch in the service, for Gene to decide to re-up for a further six, and that might have been that, except along the way, Gene had developed a passion for motorcycles, opening the door for fate to sideswipe him in a unquestionably epic manner. Legend now kicks in big time, immortalising how he blew a sizeable chunk of his reenlistment bonus on a 500cc Triumph Tiger, similar to the one ridden by Marlon Brando in *The Wild One*. One weekend in July 1955, in the Norfolk suburb of Franklin, a woman in a Chrysler ran a red light and smashed into Gene on his Triumph, crushing his left leg on impact, and changing the entire direction of his existence.

Gene was no more use to the Navy, and it looked as though he might spend the greater part of his life in and out of VA hospitals. Legend insists that doctors wanted to amputate the leg, but both he and his mother fought tooth and nail that he keep it. In a foreshadowing of lawsuits to come, Gene is also supposed to have signed some chump-change, out of court settlement with attorneys for the women in the Chrysler, who shoved the paperwork under his nose while he was out of his mind on morphine.

Gene Vincent's injured left leg looms large in both legend and reality. Like some leather-jacket Achilles, he was a hero betrayed by his own mortal form. His body became a ball and chain. Constantly braced when not in a cast, the leg – probably beyond help from the get-go – dictated his unique stage stance. It provided him a massive biker credibility, and limitless sympathy. It also tipped him into the drug and alcohol problems that would dog him for the rest of his days. Red Gwynn, his chauffeur during the first surge of fame, tells the story that would be repeated endlessly down the years. 'Gene was his own worst enemy. He popped a lot of pills... He'd break his cast in every town. Then, in the next town, we'd have to hunt up a doctor and get a new cast.'

The leg caused Gene chronic pain and quickly led to a painkiller habit and worse; the painkillers made him slow so he took speed to get back in gear; the speed made him edgy and thus he drank to mellow out. In the morning, he'd wake with a hangover and his leg still hurt. The cycle was repeated on a daily basis, a process that gradually eroded his heath, talent and stability.

Gene Vincent's crippled leg and Elvis Presley's well-known boyhood obsession with the early comic book superhero Capt Marvel Jr provide an odd and early piece of pop-culture symbolism. The premise of Captain Marvel Jr was that the crippled orphan boy Freddy Freeman utters the words of power, the magic lightning crashes down, and he his transformed into powerful and somewhat delinquent-looking Capt Marvel Jr. The allegory might be that Elvis was stuck by the magic lightning and elevated to the paranormal while Gene Vincent limped to a darker and more limited, but maybe more dignified notoriety, right here on earth, keeping it real, so to speak.

But all that was still to come. Back at the beginning, in the wake of the accident, no one was drawing any parallels with Elvis or playing with fancy comic hero analogies. Gene was just another banged-up young sailor who spent almost six months in the Portsmouth Naval Hospital, and then went back home to further convalesce. With medical benefits and Navy sick pay, Gene had some change in his jeans and time on his hands. Legend has Gene playing guitar for his messmates on the USS Chuckawan, but otherwise any musical efforts or ambitions seem to have been minimal. Any interest in music as a profession, or even a way of life, seems only to have solidified after radio station WCMS brought *The Hank Snow All Star Jamboree* to the Norfolk Municipal Auditorium, and Gene was in the crowd. Featured on the bill, along with Cowboy

Copas and the Louvin Brothers, were Elvis Presley and the Blue Moon Boys, and the spectacle of Elvis in all his raw, young majesty, at the very least started Gene Craddock thinking. In rare interview Gene, himself admits, 'I wasn't influenced by his (Elvis') voice, except that he was obviously a young kid like me.'

Through the winter of 1955/6 Gene appears to have put some kind of rock 'n' roll act together, because February of 1956 sees him entering a talent contest at the same WCMS for a regular spot on a radio show called *Country Showtime*, a provincial copy of Nashville's *Grand Ole Opry*, and winning hands down by performing of his own cover of 'Heartbreak Hotel.' Through the spring of 1956, Gene seems to have been a headliner on *Country Showtime*, and so popular that WCMS were forced to move the live recording from the Gates Theatre in Portsmouth to larger venue in Norfolk because of the size of the crowds showing up to see him. Again we have a divergence between the legend and the still-available facts. Far from being plucked from obscurity by Capitol records, Gene Vincent was actually quite the local hero in the early part of 1956. WCMS DJ Joe Hoppell recalls, 'Gene was mobbed by girls even before he made records.'

Willy Williams leader of the Virginians who were Gene's WCMS backing band confirms that Gene was knocking them dead at these shows in Norfolk. 'He came up wearing a cast, and sang 'Be-Bop-A-Lula', and the chicks went berserk.' Gene also was in the grip of his own berserk fever. 'He played guitar and fell on one knee, and slammed the mike against the floor and broke it. But he could sing like a bird, an unbelievable boy.'

And by mention of Gene's greatest hit, Williams also makes clear that Gene was road testing 'Be-Bop-A-Lula' well before even a demo had been cut.

It's quite a funny story. I was in the Naval Hospital, actually I was crippled up; I just had a hit [wound] in Korea. My mother said *to me: 'Son, why don't you enter this contest?' I said, what bloody contest, what are you talking about? She said, why don't you record something. So I recorded a thing that I wrote. I come in dead drunk and stumbled over the bed. And me and Don Graves were looking at this bloody book; it was called 'Little Lulu'. And I said, 'Hell, man, it's 'Be-Bop-a-Lulu.' And he said, 'Yeah, man, swinging.' And we wrote this song. And some man came to hear it... named Sheriff Tex Davis, and he bought the song from Donald Graves for $25. $25 dollars! So I recorded the song and told all my friends that I was going to get a Cadillac; 'cause all rock and roll singers had Cadillacs. So 'Be Be-Bop-A-Lula' came out and for three weeks nothing happened. Then some man in Baltimore started playing it and that bloody thing hit. It went to number one in every bloody place you went. But I didn't know how to handle a hit. I was only a child... a boy.*

Gene Vincent, 1970

According to the now absurdly detailed
annals of Elvis, Elvis Presley, Bill Black and
Scotty Moore first heard Gene Vincent
singing 'Be-Bop-A-Lula' on the car radio
while travelling between gigs. Bass player Bill
Black – consistently portrayed as both jealous
and paranoid that he had been left holding
the mega-star's coattails, doomed to a weekly
sideman's paycheck and second choice of the
women, rather than finding fame in his right
– immediately saw an issue for the taking,
and accused Elvis of moonlighting with
another band, on another label, and under an
assumed name. Black's contention was that
Elvis, not content with making all the money
and receiving all the attention as himself, had
invented an alter-ego with the unlikely name
Gene Vincent on which to base a entire
second clandestine career. The theory was so
psychotically absurd that Elvis, hardly
believing what he was hearing, instantly
denied it. He had his work more than cut out
being Elvis Presley. Black, however, whose
neck was reputedly as stiff as it was red,
wouldn't let it go. He continued the

argument even when Elvis pointed the obvious vocal dissimilarities; that Vincent's range was considerably higher than his and that, where he, Elvis, was influenced by the likes of Dean Martin and The Inkspots, this Vincent character, although singing rock, was straight out of the Hank Williams' school of degenerate, cousin-marrying country.

'Be-Bop-A-Lula' will always be the song most closely associated with Gene Vincent. It became his trademark, and, on stage, it was his piece de resistance. It was covered by John Lennon, the Everly Brothers, and Jeff Beck, to name but three. The genesis of the song, however, is maybe one of the most confusing episodes in the deep confusion of the whole Gene Vincent saga. As the fan magazines of the time told it, Gene was resting up in his hospital bed, fooling around with a guitar, and, inspired by the newspaper strip cartoon *Little Lulu*, he magically came up the song 'Be-Bop-A-Lula'. The kids I knew were not overly impressed by the tale, if only because *Little Lulu* was about the dumbest, blandest, and most unfunny cartoon to ever make it into the Sunday funnies. But fan mags could not always be believed. In those mid-fifties, early days, some rags even circulated patriotic, but wholly untrue stories that Gene's leg had been injured in the Korean War, and we knew that wasn't the case.

The matter of Sheriff Tex Davis was also something of a puzzlement. The name appeared on the purple label of the Capitol 45 of 'Be-Bop-A-Lula/Woman Love' as clear co-writer of the A side. So who the hell, we wondered, was this strange law enforcement officer? Had he sat at Gene's beside and co-written the song? Some rockers, already wise in the ways of the music business, passed along the rumour that Gene had parted with 50% of his hit to get himself out of some legal bind, maybe to spring himself from the jailhouse where he was being held for statutory rape or public intoxication. This was no more true than the *Little Lulu* story, but it fitted a whole lot better with the image. In fact, Bill 'Sheriff Tex' Davis, was a chubby would-be music mogul, wheeling and dealing in the Norfolk area, who had a taste for cowboy outfits, and fancied himself as a potential rival to Colonel Tom Parker. Davis had manoeuvred himself into the role of Gene's manager shortly after the WCMS talent contest. Nothing indicates that he was ever the legitimate sheriff of anywhere, and the title may have been honorary, like Parker's rank of Colonel, or simply Davis's own invention.

The sad truth may well be that neither Gene nor Davis had anything to do with the writing of the song. Dickie Harrell, who, at fifteen, was the first drummer with The Blue Caps, tells a different story, with a certain credibility if only because Harrell would have little reason to lie. 'Actually the song was written by a guy from Portsmouth named Donald Graves.' Vincent and his first manager, brought the tune outright for 25 bucks. 'It happened a lot in those days. Guys would take the sure money.'

At this point, it might be well to remember that, back in these formative days of rock 'n' roll, the business in no way resembled the global and corporate media empire it is today. Elvis notwithstanding, rock was considered the hula-hoop of the music business, and was fully expected to burnout in a matter of months. Rock & roll was a carnival, and hustlers and huckster like Colonel Parker and Sheriff Davis saw young talent like Presley and Vincent as maybe the source of a big fast score, but hardly artists whose legacy would extend into the next century, whose music would still be heard and discussed some fifty years after its release, and the accuracy of the accounts of their life and work scrutinized and questioned. Whether the rough and tumble rip-offs and fairground exploitation of those wild and wooly early years of rock 'n' roll were helpful or detrimental to the music continues to be debated to this day. Would Gene Vincent have lived longer and achieved more without the procession of fast-buck managers, starting with Bill Davis, or, without the crude sleight-of-hand, and the deals from the bottom of the deck? Or would he have merely remained a local hero playing honky-tonks around Norfolk, Virginia and it's environs? After all this time, the answer can only be a matter of speculation. No argument, however, that the tradition of swindling managers, chaotic private and public lives, and performers who died young and left a wasted corpse was firmly in place well before Gene came on the scene.

When Hank Williams Sr, the first real superstar of country music, died aged 29, in the back of his baby blue Cadillac on the way to a 1952 New Year's Eve show in Canton, Ohio, he was killed by the time-honoured combination of the booze and barbiturates he was swilling and popping to come down off the speed that was keeping him on the road. His death created a romantic tradition of self-destructive genius that Gene Vincent was neither the first, nor, by far, the last, unconsciously to emulate. Hank Williams is up there with Woody Guthrie, Chuck Berry, and Bob Dylan, an immortal among American song writers, but, on a more prosaic, day to day level, he was a mess.

He formed his first band The Drifting Cowboys at age fourteen and by fifteen was reputed to have become a full blown, binge-drinking alcoholic. Later he would graduate to Benzedrine and chloral hydrate. Like Gene, he dragged around a crippling physical disability that added chronic pain to the equation of booze and drugs. Hank's spine was deformed by childhood spina bifida. His marriage to his first wife, Audrey Mae Sheppard Guy, performed in a gas station in Andalusia, Alabama was a combination of a hurricane and a nightmare, while his second to teenager Billie Jean Jones, was a disaster of shorter duration, with the nuptials happening just two and a half months before Hank's death, culminating in him being too drunk to make it to his own honeymoon in the then wide-open Havana, Cuba. After his death the two wives fought over his legacy, with Billie Jean at a considerable disadvantage, having neglected to divorce a previous husband before becoming Mrs Williams.

Although Nashville now claims Hank Williams as one of its high pantheon, the country music establishment hated him while he was alive. Hank rose to fame on the Grand Ole Opry, and at his debut show, was called back for no less than six encores, but he was permanently banned from this cathedral of country just three years later even though his records like 'Lovesick Blues', 'Why Don't You Love Me', and 'Cold Cold Heart' consistently made the top ten and stayed there for weeks on end. The overt reasons were that he was a drunken, unreliable, no-show son-of-a-bitch who had been caught with too much underage jailbait, had shot up too many hotel rooms, and even set fire to a few when he nodded out with a cigarette in his hand. But country had plenty of other rowdies, drunks, and fuck-ups who were never excommunicated like Hank, and the deeper reason was that he injected a sexual energy – plus a trace mixing of the blues he'd learned from his boyhood black mentor Tee-Tot – into his version of country, making it, in every way, a foreshadowing of the rock 'n' roll that was shortly to come. Hank Williams scared the shit out of Nashville in the late 1940s and early 1950s, but greasy pool hall punks with pegged pants and turned-up collars like Gene Vincent and Elvis Presley watched him in awe.

Gene may have only recorded two of Hank's compositions – 'Your Cheating Heart' and 'Hey Good Looking', and made passing reference, in early bubblegum fan mag interviews, to how Hank was an early influence, but, both in his music and also his behaviour, Gene was a natural inheritor of the Hank Williams' legacy, and he knew it. Both had a high range vocal palette, both used the tricks and phrasing of bluegrass high lonesome, except Gene adapted it to a world of TV sets and Ford Thunderbirds. In their youth they shared the same, hollowed eyed, white-trash look of desperate emaciation, and both were totally unable to cope with their demons, except by drowning then out with booze and pills and the howl of electric guitars.

I'm a singer, man. When I put out a record called 'Be Be-Bop-A-Lula', my only thought was to just make a living singing. But all of a sudden, I was getting $1,500 a night. And you take a 19-year old boy and put him in those circumstances... I had a Cadillac and all. It was a bad scene. It shouldn't have happened on that first record.

Gene Vincent, 1970

On June 16th 1956, 'Be-Bop-A-Lula' entered the Billboard Hot Hundred, but not before another bout of the random chaos that seemed to shadow Gene Vincent's every move. While Gene was headlining on *Country Showtime*, Bill Davis began the process of wheeling and dealing to make some money off his phenomenal discovery. One of the Sheriff's most powerful contacts was Capitol Records' head of country music A&R, Ken Nelson, and when Davis made the call, the timing could not have been more fortuitous. Elvis had signed with RCA and Capitol was in the process of looking for a rock 'n' roll contender of their own. The call was followed by a demo cut at WCMS, and after a tense three-week delay, Gene and a band comprised of Willie Williams of the Virginians, Jack Neal on bass, Dickie Harrell on drums, and newly recruited guitarist called Cliff Gallup were flown to Nashville to cut four tracks: 'Be-Bop-A-Lula', 'Woman Love', 'Race With The Devil', and 'I Sure Miss You' on May 4th with Owen Bradley. The sessions had a definite potential for disaster since Bradley was an old school Nashville studio boss who ran his sessions like a fiddle-and-guitar dictatorship. Previously he had overseen sessions that so diluted Buddy Holly's work, Holly had angrily fled back to his hometown of Lubbock, Texas, vowing that he'd rather record in his own garage than ever again be straitjacketed by the Nashville system.

The plus for Gene and the band came in the form of engineer Mort Thomasson, who had built a slapback echo system in Bradley's studio that he believed rivalled the set-up that Sam Phillips had at Sun Studios down in

Memphis and, having heard what was being done with Elvis Presley, was anxious to shake down the tech on some of this new rock 'n' roll everyone was talking about. Although initially daunted by the fact that Gene and his crew were sitting round in black jackets, and reminded him of a 'motorcycle gang', Thomasson's contribution should never be underestimated. The major minus was the chance that only Gene himself might be performing on the actual recordings. Ken Nelson had lined up Nashville aces Buddy Harmon, Grady Martin, Hank Garland, and Bob Moore, who would be able to step in and take over when Gene and his band of untried studio neophytes failed to hack a major label session. Although Gene had been asked to bring his band to Nashville, both Nelson and Owen Bradley saw Cliff Gallup and the rest of the future Blue Caps as wholly expendable, but expendability ceased when Gallup began to pick guitar all over the first tune on the list, 'Race With The Devil'. The hired-gun country aces might not have been fully aware that a rock 'n' roll legend had slouched in to be born, but they knew the kids had a party started, and all they could bring to the table was wholly inappropriate grown up expertise.

Harmon, Martin, Garland, and Moore told Ken Nelson that they going for a beer, and history was allowed to take its course. When the session men had left the building, and – in complete opposition to all the current rules of recording – the Blue Caps played loud, so loud in fact that Mort Thomasson had a hard time setting a voice level on Gene. The only answer was to move Gene out into the studio stairway with his mike, the door propped open with a Coca-Cola crate, and the mix from the board coming to him through headphones. Thomasson may have rigged the first vocal isolation booth in country music, as Gene moved Nashville into rock 'n' roll.

History never has everything its own way, and even in the very Book of Genesis, the Gene Vincent story has more than its share of near misses. Initially, the debut single was to have been the gasping, grinding 'Woman

Love', with 'Be-Bop-A-Lula' on the B-side. Advance promo on 'Woman Love', however, ran into a massive wall of resistance from radio stations all across the USA, plus an outright ban in Great Britain by the BBC. Elvis was bad enough, but 'Woman Love', with it's overt sexual rage and frustration, and Gene's near orgasmic breathing on the slap-echo vocal track, was ten times worse. No way was 'Woman Love' 1950s radio friendly, reinforcing as it did the popular prejudice the rock 'n' roll would trigger 'promiscuity, delinquency and the mixing of the races'.

Then a Baltimore DJ flipped the record and started playing 'Be-Bop-A-Lula'. Capitol quickly followed suit and switched the emphasis. 'Be-Bop-A-Lula' became the A-side, and, once again, history continued.

History also cut deeper than just Capitol Records and the Billboard Top Forty. With this very first single, 'Be-Bop-A-Lula'/ 'Woman Love', Gene had communicated directly to millions of malcontent kids across the planet that he was somehow subversive.

The quivering breathlessness and the near loss of control at the end of the verses in 'Be-Bop-A-Lula', drummer Dickie Harrell's primal scream in the first verse, the uncompromising guitar solo from Cliff Gallup, that John Lennon would honour on his cover of the song by playing note for note, all given an unholy and desperate edge by Mort Thomasson's slapback echo system, added up to a pent-up – but unrepentant – sexual rage that might, at any second, apocalyptically break loose. And then, on the other side of the vinyl, 'Woman Love', was another helping of the same, only more so. 'Woman Love' was the built-in forbidden fruit that made the disk even more tantalising. The global teenage grapevine relished the tale of how 'Woman Love' had been banned from the radio, and concluded that it must be somehow dangerous – and therefore to be desired. With 'Be-Bop-A-Lula', the tolerated and the proscribed came in the single package.

To ban 'Woman Love', and then promote the other side of the record was clearly absurd, and it didn't seem to occur to the guardians of morality that the two or more million kids who ultimately bought the record after its first release would hear 'Woman Love' anyway, and cherish it as their private dirty secret.

The Capitol promotion department had dubbed Gene, 'the Screaming End', as their answer to the loathsome Elvis the Pelvis nickname, but, in the sometimes mind-numbing cultural repression of the 1950's, juvenile delinquents, rightly or wrongly, had convinced themselves, on the strength of this first forty-five, that Gene Vincent was one of their own. Elvis Presley might be hailed as the monarch, but Gene Vincent guarded the dark heart of rock 'n' roll, a pale-faced, limping and black-clad gangster-Gollum, who carried the real Ring of Power.

I went to Nashville. I walked in the door of the Prince Albert Hotel and had on a pink suit with a wine-coloured shirt. See, they hated me right from the start, cause I had the number one record in town. But I didn't know that at the time. So I went to this big disk-jockeys' convention in town and a person was playing there by the name of Bill Monroe. He had a bluegrass band. And everybody was sitting there. Then Faron Young got up and said: 'There's this fella in town; one of these rock and roll people who's only going to last a year, if he lasts that long. But by the way he sings, he won't.' And then he said: 'And there sits the boy. He might sing in a minute. His name is Gene Vincent.' And man, I snuck out that door ... crawled out of there. He brought me down so bad! So I went back to the hotel and there was this fella sitting there in the lobby who came up to me and said, 'Excuse me, can I get your autograph?' And I said, 'Haven't I seen you someplace before?' And he said, 'Yeah, my name's Buddy Holly.' He had out a record then called 'Blue Days, Black Nights'. It was a fabulous record.

Gene Vincent, 1970

Chapter Two

'GLOBE, ARIZONA WAS another wild gig and it soon erupted into a full scale riot. A fight broke out when Gene was dragged from the stage by the local sheriff in the middle of doing "Lotta Lovin". They had to shoot teargas into the joint. Navahos and Apaches were going at it.' Tommy Facenda, one of the original 'Clapper Boys, part back-up singers, part dancers, part sinister hoodlum figures, who flanked Gene during his 1950s show tells stories of what came to pass when the Blue Caps went out on the road in the first flash of real stardom. Rhythm guitarist, Grady Owen, tells much the same story in Britt Hagarty's Vincent biography *The Day The World Turned Blue*. 'The sheriff had arrested Gene for wrecking a motel room, being drunk around minors and doing a lewd show. They dragged him off stage bodily and took him to jail. The whole thing erupted so the sheriff came back and shot teargas bombs in the place and cleared it.' Paul Peek, the second Clapper Boy, adds a slightly different dimension to the incident. 'Some Pachuccos mouth off to me and Bubba (Tommy Facenda) and I'd said a few things back, which maybe I shouldn't have. But they swore they were going to come back and get us. We were on stage doing 'Lotta Lovin'', and we were down on our knees singing, and the place was going crazy. Then a fight broke out and suddenly everyone was fighting. It was like the place exploded.' And Peek agrees with the same eventual outcome. 'So the sheriff's deputies came and got us, and took us to a room backstage, and shot off a bunch of teargas. It was wild.' And when the wildness abated, the band had to wire Dallas for money to pay Gene's bail.

The accepted history of rock 'n' roll generally creates the impression that riots, arrests, teargas, and wrecked motels were the business of the 1960s and 1970s. Chaos and disorder started with The Who, The Doors, and were perpetuated by The Clash, The Sex Pistols, and Marilyn Manson.

These contemporary accounts make it clear that Gene Vincent and his guitar wielding 'motorcycle gang' were dogged by violence, and mayhem ten years before Iggy ever slashed his own chest, taunted outlaw bikers, hurled peanut butter, or walked on the hands of the crowd. Ken Nelson at Capitol began to realize that Gene very definitely wasn't Elvis, and to understand just exactly where 'the Screaming End' might really be located. Where Elvis would prove to be polite and hopelessly malleable, Gene turned out to be wilful, difficult, often drunk, and possibly a little insane. Where Elvis attempted to be all things to all people, Gene conformed to the classic description once applied to the poet Lord Byron. He was 'mad, bad, and dangerous to know'. There were times when Capitol undoubtedly would have preferred to drop Gene from its roster of artists, but he was their rock 'n' roll white hope, and, even though, his second single 'Race With The Devil' was not a hit, 'Be-Bop-A-Lula' had remained on the charts for almost six months, and his third single, 'Bluejean Bop', went gold. Another odd phenomenon had also come into play. Gene Vincent sold albums.

Gene and the Blue Caps had started work on their first album less than two months after the sessions that had turned out 'Be-Bop-A-Lula'. In the early days of rock, albums were all too often makeshift affairs, and many were nothing short of deceptive packaging; just a couple of hits and their attendant B-sides wrapped around with a whole lot of crap filler, with a colour picture of the star on the cover. By the second half of the 1950s, the major record companies accepted that their classical labels sold albums, jazz labels sold albums, and smaller independents like Chess were able to move blues and R&B LPs by Chuck Berry, Muddy Waters and Howling Wolf. Perry Como sold albums, Capitol were well aware that Frank Sinatra sold albums, but rock 'n' rollers didn't sell albums. Sure Elvis Presley was the exception. Elvis sold albums, but Elvis could sell anything. Even in those comparatively simple days Elvis's image was on every kind of merchandise with the exception of a Pez dispenser. Gene's first album *Bluejean Bop* was hardly distinguished. The best that could be said of it was that it didn't recycle 'Be-Bop-A-Lula', 'Woman Love', 'Race With The Devil', and 'I Sure Miss You'. In addition to the title track, it contained a just handful of new rock and roll recordings, 'Who Slapped John?', 'Jump Back Honey, Jump Back', and 'Jumps Giggles And Shouts, plus a melodramatic reading of the standard 'Jezebel', but far too much of it was totally pointless schlock filler, and it's hard to image what greasy punk wanted to hear Gene Vincent croon his way through 'Peg O' My Heart' or 'Waltz Of The Wind.'

Despite the poverty of the content though, *Bluejean Bop* sold considerably better than the average slapped-together LP by a supposed one hit wonder, and although record companies of the time did not exactly analyse demographics, Gene seemed to sell more to boys than girls, confirming what I would observe at the Brighton Essoldo a few years later.

The second album, *Gene Vincent and the Blue Caps*, proved to be a quantum improvement over *Bluejean Bop*. Although again recorded in a fast four days at Own Bradley's studio in Nashville, the material was bright, new, and intense, and Gene and guitarist Cliff Gallup, working together for what would be the last time, created the sound of a tight, honed, and fully coordinated band at work. The collaboration had no hint of just a singer and an assembly of sidemen – so often the case with the majority of fifties rock idols. Instead – although no one was to know it – *Gene Vincent and the Blue Caps* was a full precursor of the closeness and musical familiarity that was the hallmark of the groups of the 1960s. At the time, no one wrote reviews of rock 'n' roll albums. Reviews in print were for Miles Davis, not Gene Vincent.

No one in the media articulated the power of the effort, and only teenage fans recognised a masterwork, as Gallup and Vincent locked on 'Red Blue Jeans And A Ponytail', 'Cruisin' 'Pink Thunderbird', and reached a near pathological peak with the sinister 'Cat Man', or when the Jordaniares were hired away from Elvis for the day to add the finishing touches to the ballad 'Important Words'.

Forty-six years later, the magazine *Mojo* would nominate *Gene Vincent and the Blue Caps* as one of its *100 Greatest Guitar Albums* with the comment: 'Gallup's pioneering techniques for devising ringing reverb and vibrato helped set the blueprint for the classic rockabilly sound'. Unfortunately, at the same time as *Gene Vincent and the Blue Caps* was blazing its trail, another, more negative blueprint was being drawn up, and the first indications of what would be the darker side of the Gene Vincent story were starting to become manifest, gathering like dark shadows of episodes to come.

When I entered music, music was a fantastic thing. It was a competition; we all competed with each other. But since then, music has become a business... it's more of a competition among businessmen. You stuff things down people's throats, which they don't like, and then you say: 'Why is rock and roll coming back?' Well, rock and roll is coming back because people want the original... and, they're going to have it. The people want it!

They're not businessmen or anything... they're just people who enjoy the music. Here, I'm going to tell you something which you probably don't know about.

You've heard about this payola stuff that happened back in '58? Well, they do the same thing now. All they do is give you a Swiss number, a Swiss bank account number.

You play the record and you pick up $300 in Swiss money.

Gene Vincent, 1970

Although it is hardly mentioned in the Gene Vincent legend, Gene and the Blue Caps were among the first rockers to manage to make a positive mark in Las Vegas. In April 1956, Elvis Presley had been booked into the main room of the New Frontier and had died an humiliating death. Teenagers were excluded from the main room of the casino, and the gamblers either didn't get Elvis and his hillbilly cat act, or else they actively hated him.

When Gene played the Sands Hotel in October of the same year, right after recording *Gene Vincent and the Blue Caps*, a different strategy was employed. Drummer Dickie Harrell, one of the last remaining witnesses to the early days explains: 'They didn't put us in the main ballroom because we were a fill-in act. We played the Sands lounge, the midnight shift, twelve to six. We played forty minutes, and were off for twenty. For a whole two weeks it was jammed in there, every night it was jammed. They'd never seen anything like it before and the people would eat it up.'

In fact, the people were eating it to such an extent that the Sands expressed some displeasure that Gene was actually pulling gamblers away from the craps and blackjack, but, despite this impediment to cash-flow, the New Frontier management wanted to hold him over for a further three weeks. Gene, however, was not about to re-up for Vegas. The damage being done to his injured leg by the Sands' forty minutes on and twenty minutes off, coming as it did on top of recording sessions, and a protracted stint on the road, simply could not be ignored. Once more in a plaster cast, his leg started to bleed regularly, and it was clear to everyone that Gene needed a long rest after the events of 1956. He was in no condition to perform, or even, as it turned out, to hold the Blue Caps together. By the end of the residency at the Sands, Cliff Gallup had already begged off spending any more time on the road, figuring that a travelling rock band, exposed to cops, teargas and drunken Pachuccos, was no place for a man with a family. Seeing that Gene was going nowhere except maybe into a hospital, bass player Jack Neal also quit. More importantly, an irreparable rift had developed between Gene and Sheriff Tex Davis, and the inevitable lawyers were moving into the picture. Whether the split with Davis can be viewed as a blessing in disguise, sorting out the threat of litigation between artist and manager did provide Gene with an enforced break during which he was minimally able to rest his leg and receive treatment that was more than emergency room first aid.

The spell off the road, on the other hand, was no rock star vacation. Although 1956 had taken Gene to places beyond even the wilder dreams of a skinny white sailor with a damaged leg, the year drew to a close with his life in considerable disarray. He was without management, the combo that had given him 'Be-Bop-A-Lula' was in fragments, and the sole remaining Blue Cap was Dickie

Harrell. The working relationship with Cliff
Gallup was sundered, and Gene could have
been forgiven for lapsing into a serious back-
to-square-one depression. He was, however,
still young and resilient. He still had a deal
with Capitol and little alternative but to
recruit a number two version of the Blue
Caps, unless he wanted to lapse into making
records with day-labour, hired-gun sidemen,
and with Ken Nelson calling all of the shots.
Paul Peek who had replaced Willie Williams
on rhythm guitar for *Gene Vincent and the
Blue Caps*, introduced Gene to a guitarist
from South Carolina called Johnny Meeks,
who, while no Cliff Gallup, had more than
adequate chops to fill the slot. Meeks brought
Bill Mack to the party to cover the bass, and
suddenly things didn't seem too bad after all.

While rebuilding the Blue Caps, the
concept of the Clapper Boys seems to have
occurred to Gene. Where performers Ray
Charles and Ike Turner would spice up a live
show with girl back-up singers in short, tight
dresses, and with coordinated bump & grind
choreography, Gene seemed to understand

instinctively that his appeal was all about the motorcycle gang, *The Magnificent Seven*, and *The Three Musketeers*, not some hot, sequined-and-sexy R&B revue. Accordingly he organized himself a duo of boy back-up singers in the persons of Paul Peek, who he moved away from the second guitar, and a buddy of Dickie Harrell, who went by the name of Tommy 'Bubba' Facenda, and sported the do-wop Italian good looks of Tony Soprano's father. Those who actually witnessed a show with the Clapper Boys describe it as crude rock 'n' roll theatre, *West Side Story* before its time. After the band had performed a couple of warm-up numbers, Gene and the Clapper Boys would loom on together, simultaneous and menacing, then Peek and Facenda would stand close on either side of Gene doing a synchronized Elvis, throwing dramatic, dark-alley shapes while Gene went progressively insane. Homoerotic? Maybe, but who gave a rat's ass? Wouldn't Dr. Feelgood employee the same shtick twenty years later on their 'Riot In Cell Block #9' finale? Since the dawn of time, ape-man to Masai, Samurai to modern riot police, all cultures have featured the young male's display of aggression, and Gene had merely set it to 'Who Slapped John?', and 'Rolling Danny'. A probably toned-down version of Gene and the Clapper Boys is preserved in the 'Baby Blue' sequence from the movie 'Hot Rod Gang', and maybe, ultimately, some conglomerate will have the wit to release the clip on DVD if we wait long enough.

It may also have been male aggression that initially attracted Eddie Cochran to the orbit of Gene and the Blue Caps.

Eddie Cochran could be described as an accessible Elvis clone. His voice didn't have the mighty resonance, and his looks were not so Michelangelo perfect. He was more the hood-next-door, except the hood-next-door also happened to be something of a nascent genius who played advanced guitar, and, like Buddy Holly, was a self-taught innovator in the recording studio, creating early pop effects with shoe box percussion, tambourines, electric and acoustic guitars, crude over-dubs and home made echo systems, and had either Cochran, Holly, or both, lived though the 1960s, either might have been competing with Phil Spector or even Frank Zappa. Eddie Cochran was born in Oklahoma, raised in Minnesota, then moved to California with his family, late-arriving Okies in Woodie Guthrie's promised land. Like every picker from Fresno to Bakersfield, Eddie Cochran (originally Cochrane) went into country music, teaming, at the tender age of sixteen, with singer-guitarist Hank Cochran (no relation), and then touring and recording as the Cochran Brothers. Cochran cut his first rock record, 'Skinny Jim', for the Crest label in July 1956, and the song contained the reverential line *'be-bop-a-lula, Skinny Jim'*, referring to Gene's hit that was, at the time, high in the charts. Signed to the more viable Liberty label, and in just four short years, he would go on to write at least three all-time rock classics, 'Twenty Flight Rock', 'Summertime Blues', and 'Something Else', that have been

covered by everyone from Blue Cheer, to Sid
Vicious, to The Who.

Debate continues just exactly how and
when Gene Vincent and Eddie Cochran
hooked up. Legend used to have it that they
met up while both Vincent and Cochran were
filming song sequences for the Jayne
Mansfield movie *The Girl Can't Help It*. The
idea of their meeting on a movie set has a
Hollywood plausibility, but according to
Dickie Harrell, the friendship was really
cemented at *The Rock & Roll Jubilee Of
Stars*, a week long, proto rock festival in
Philadelphia at which both men had been
given star billing. 'Eddie was just down-to-
earth and really good people. He and Gene
had a lot in common. They were a bit like
each other and seemed to understand each
other. So they started to pal around together.'

This palling around continued through a
package tour of Australia headlined by
Vincent, Cochran and Little Richard, who
recalls: 'I had toured with Gene Vincent and
Eddie Cochran in Australia in 1957. Gene
was a good friend of mine, but he was an

annoying fella sometimes. I remember Gene
would get drunk and want to put you out of
the car while you were travelling along the
highway. I thought he was totally mad when
he'd had some drink.' While Vincent and
Richard engaged in regular bouts of butting
egos – and the launch of Sputnik, plus a bad
flight through an outback thunderstorm also
highly unnerved Richard, who was on the
verge of his first renunciation of rock, and his
first seeking of refuge in Jesus – Gene and
Cochran remained friends and drinking
buddies, often joining each other on stage to
close their respective sets. Certainly the
friendship and musical understanding had
blossomed to the point that, in March 1958,
when Gene was recording his fourth album,
Gene Vincent Record Date, in the basement
of Hollywood's Capitol Tower, Cochran felt
able to drop by and join Facenda and Peek,
singing a third line bass back-up, handling
the deep do-wop counterpoint on the classic
'Git It'.

In a world that is all too often blinded by
an obsession with guitars and guitar heroes,

the crucial part played by back-up vocals in
the music of Gene Vincent has been largely
overlooked. From about 1958 onwards, the
arrangements became more lavish, and back-
up vocals took an increasingly important
role. On some tracks like 'Peace Of Mind'
and the classic 'Git It' with the basso refrain
well-oh-well-oh-wop-wip-wip-wip, Vincent
actually started to stray cross culturally close
to New York do-wop, the turf of which Dion
and the Belmonts were masters, and Cochran,
if not an instigator, was certainly a source of
confidence as Gene attempted to expand and
deepen his recorded sound.

Sparse, atmospheric rockabilly was bulked
up to a more elaborate and much denser rock
'n' roll, without making the usual concessions
to the kind of multi-layered pop so freely
embraced by Elvis and Buddy Holly. The
song 'Baby Blue', recorded in 1957 for the
low budget teen exploitation movie *Hot Rod
Gang* (released in Britain under the title *Fury
Unleashed*), is the perfect example of
Vincent's evolution to a more constructed
approach to a rock sound. In what was

essentially a deluxe-and-loaded second look at 'Heartbreak Hotel', Vincent went for pounding percussion, that broke with the traditional rockabilly snare and high hat. The mood was locked by threatening piano triplets and a heavy overlay of back-up vocals chanting 'baby-baby-baby-baby', until an almost hypnotic pulse was achieved. In a 1970 *Rolling Stone* retrospective on Vincent, Simon Firth sums up Gene's approach to rock 'n' roll when he was at his best. 'The interplay of voices and instruments are perfect, the total effect being built up by the between conflict of all the elements... these tracks quite transcended the normal rock 'n' roll singles of 1957-8.'

The sound expanded, a tentative link was forged with Eddie Cochran, and after two singles that failed to make an appreciable dent in the charts, Gene was back in the top ten hit with 'Lotta Lovin". He even made it to the *Ed Sullivan Show*, and rumors have always circulated that a tape existed of the prestigious national TV show, but it has never surfaced. Although Gene's life appeared set fair, complications were on the horizon.

Ken Nelson had signed Gene to a new management deal with the McLemore Agency, and he and the Blue Caps were touring constantly. So constantly that, by 1958, the strain was plain. Dickie Harrell started to burn out, and was replaced by the even younger Juvie Gomez. Peek and Facenda were also tugging at the leash, speculating about solo careers of their own. Johnny Meek left the band, and it began to seem as Gene was having trouble holding together an unchanging and viable version of the Blue Caps for more than a few months at a time. He publically complained in an interview with Vancouver DJ Red Robinson that 'You never meet anyone long enough to get to know them. The travelling is mostly what gets you down. It gets horrible sometimes.'

Gene may also have been contributing to his own horrors. After a tepid response to the single of the classic 'Baby Blue', those around him started to notice that the singer's drinking had not only markedly increased, but that he was using the booze to wash down increasing numbers of prescription pain pills. Clapper Boy Paul Peek recalled that Gene 'got to be more of a recluse, and he didn't want to sign autographs or give interviews. He'd stay in his hotel room and brood, and he got to thinking the world was down on him.'

Around the same time, Peek remembers Gene started exhibiting an unhealthy obsession with firearms. 'Gene pulled a gun and clicked it at us once. We were leaving the hotel early in the morning and piling into the car. There'd been a party the night before, and we were all laughing. Then Gene swung around and said, 'Laugh at me, will you, you bastards!' So he pulled this gun out. Thacker yelled at him, 'You stupid son-of-a-bitch! Put that damn thing away!' Afterwards, Gene felt a bit sheepish about it because it turned out that there was a damned bullet in the gun. It could have been fatal.'

And if close-to-hand problems weren't enough, the larger world was turning increasingly complicated as conservative

America mounted its first counter-offensive against the subversion of rock 'n' roll. The radio payola scandals, and tales of DJs accepting cash and gifts in return for plugging selected rock records made lurid headlines, and the resulting congressional and senate investigations would resemble nothing less than a rock 'n' roll witch hunt. Almost all of the first generation of rockers would find themselves tainted: Alan Freed – the man who claimed to have coined the phase 'rock 'n' roll' in the first place – would go to jail for accepting bribes, Chuck Berry would do time for pimping. Jerry Lee Lewis would sink in his personal morass of marriage scandals. Elvis was already safely out of it in the Army, and Little Richard was on the point of deciding that maybe he was better off preaching. The cross that Gene had to bear was a ruthless IRS tax audit which stripped him of his home and most of his possessions. Gene, who had never been too precise at handling money or keeping records had rather naively assumed that the McLemore Agency was paying his taxes along with his other expenses. This had not been the case, and Gene found himself owing the US government in excess of $50,000 dollars – closer to a half million in today's terms. When he couldn't come up with a cash settlement, the Feds moved in and seized the large house in Dallas that he had bought only a year or so earlier.

Although, on one level, Gene only had himself to blame for his troubles, they were also a sign of the times. The government believed it had a mission to 'clean up rock 'n' roll', and even run the godless and subversive movement out of town. And if it took tax audits and going through financial records with a fine tooth comb, so be it. The payola outcry was matched by the parallel scandals over fixed TV quiz shows, and no less than President Dwight Eisenhower demanded a shake-up of what he saw as a highly corrupt entertainment industry. Later in life, Gene would insist that there had been a government vendetta exclusively against him, but, in fact, he was really a peripheral victim who found himself caught up in the general housecleaning, and the rest was a product of his own stoned paranoia. Paranoid or not though, he found himself all but penniless, and even had to burn The Blue Caps on their salary cheques. Gene hung on as best he could. He played Canada and spent time in the Pacific North West, playing mainly with pick-up bands.

Gene's fortunes looked up somewhat when a deal between Capitol and the consumer electronics giant Toshiba resulted in his being the very first American rocker to tour Japan and the Far East. The trip was prestigious, but nevertheless conducted on a very low budget. Gene took guitarist Jerry Merritt with him, and picked up a Japanese rhythm section, sight-unseen, when he arrived in Tokyo. The idea of Japanese Blue Caps can only conjure a bizarre cartoon absurdity, but it seems to have worked for Gene. Indeed, Japan in 1959 – full throttle into its post World War II economic miracle – seems to have been so hungry for any real-deal rock 'n' roll that Gene was received and treated in way that would not be equalled until The

Beatles landed. He and Merritt were met at Tokyo International Airport by ten thousand screaming fans, and a motorcade of limousines whisked them to the presidential suite at the Nakatsu Hotel. In back-to-back shows at the auditorium-sized Nichigeki Theatre, they played to more than a quarter of a million people. In Osaka, they filled a 40,000 seat sports arena, and were treated to the favors of a constant procession of models and starlets. The few remaining photographs of the Japanese concerts show Vincent, Merritt, and their local sidemen, raving, gesticulating, and down on their knees, ready to testify.

Unfortunately, Japan proved to be a peak that was at odds with the prevailing downward spiral. Back at home, a substandard album, *Sounds Like Gene Vincent*, had put a dent in record sales, and some of Gene's best tunes, including 'Git It' and 'She She Little Sheila' and 'Say Mama' had all tanked. He had slightly redeemed himself with the superior *Crazy Times* album, but everything about Gene seemed at odds with what was going on in the world around him. In less than four years he had become an anachronism, and the stress of what looked like slow decay and unstoppable failure was making the man hard to be around. The changes that he faced were not only a product of government intervention. Rock & roll itself was changing and being changed. On radio, a swing to a bubblegum, top-forty format was underway, and DJs colluded with the record companies to engineer the rise of safe, manufactured pop idols. Radio and TV were no longer either R&B or rockabilly friendly, opting instead for neat teen-boy crooners, in sweaters and conservative suits, and girl singers in prom dresses and bouffants. Gene even managed to alienate Dick Clarke who, since the fall of Alan Freed, had become the arbiter of what was acceptable in US pop. After showing up staggering drunk for a taping of Clarke's *American Bandstand*, Gene found himself banned and virtually blacklisted from the prestigious TV show, which had a stranglehold on national record sales. Like

Hank Williams, banned from *The Grand Old Opry* nearly a decade before, Gene was starting to find that, all round him, similar doors were closing on him.

Hey, everybody was making money 'cept me. When I was 28, I got a letter from the Government saying I was a millionaire. I wish to hell they would have told somebody else about it... like me. I never knew about it. I never had that money. In fact, I've still got about 10 checks that were signed by my manager overseas... $10,000 or so. But I don't care. I just don't care. I know it sounds silly. But look, let them take what they want. All I want to do is be myself and make a decent living.

Gene Vincent, 1970

Chapter Three

BY THE STANDARDS of British television at the end of 1959, to present a performance on a TV pop show as a full-blown mini-drama was a move in the direction of revolution, but this is exactly what happened with Gene's first appearance in England. The screen faded to black and two white words appeared – GENE VINCENT – as though an event of ominous significance was about to take place. Lights slowly came up, but, at first, all that could be seen was Joe Brown's white guitar. Then Gene was visible, clutching a mike-stand with both hands in what would, from then on, be his trademark stage posture of the hunched cripple. The rockabilly cat clothes, the high rise pants, white shoes and white belt, and reflective satin shirts that had been his routine stage outfits in the US had been banished. Gene was dressed entirely in black; black leather jacket, black jeans, black gloves. Greasy hair flopped over his forehead. His collar was turned up, creating an effect that was part Elvis, part Harley Davidson vampire. A heavy gold medallion hung from a chain around his neck. The entire image had been lifted from Laurence Olivier's 1955 movie version of *Richard III*, although it's debatable who knew, or even who cared. As Gene launched into a slow and grinding version of 'Baby Blue', a Newcastle kid called Steve Aynsley, who'd later become President of the Gene Vincent Fan Club in Great Britain, was glued to the family TV set, experiencing too much of an epiphany to spot cultural references. 'Gene picked up the mike stand and walked towards the camera until his face filled the screen. I'd never seen anything like it in my life. And I realized that nobody could ever make such an impression on me again. He wore black leather and the light faded as he moved around. He looked like a demon.'

For its time, the Granada Saturday evening rock 'n' roll show *Boy Meets Girls* had edge. Filmed in Manchester, it had been designed as ITV's countermeasure to the hearty, healthy, youth club ambience of the BBC's *Six Five Special*, that tended to feature harmless pop, good intentions, and skiffle groups. *Boy Meets Girls* had gone for all the raunch and glitz that was possible on the heavily censored medium in a heavily censorial age. Young boys across the land salivated over the *Boy Meets Girls* resident dancers, The Vernons Girls, whose tight sweaters and ultra-short shorts left as little as was permissible to the imagination. The creative drive behind the show came from its producer, Cambridge graduate Jack Good. Good, who later went on to produce early episodes of the mod TV bible *Ready, Steady, Go*, and finally made the jump to the United

States and the ABC Network to create *Shindig* and *Hullabaloo*, may have been pompous and loudly over-educated, but his instincts and perceptions were usually in the right place. In the case of Gene Vincent, he excelled himself. He accurately sensed the sinister and dangerous aura that couldn't help but surround Gene, and reached for the wild biker/Richard III combination. And, by so doing, started what, for Gene, was close to a second coming on the other side of the Atlantic.

The remaking of Gene Vincent had commenced one week earlier. As with his visit to Tokyo, he had landed at Heathrow airport to definite outbreak if Gene-mania. When he arrived on December 5th 1959, coming off the red-eye from New York in a cold mid-winter dawn, a milling reception committee of press, fans, screaming teeny-boppers, and bike-riding rockers – plus Joe Brown and the Bruvvers playing 'Be-Bop-A-Lulu' by way of a fanfare – were there to greet him. Whether the reception was orchestrated by Good or Capitol Records is not clear, but it certainly created the impression that someone of great importance had blown into town, and not a man who, after a handful of hits, was now on the lam from creditors, a bad reputation, and growing posse of his own demons. He was whisked off to a promo breakfast in the West End, a BBC interview and than a fast rehearsal with Marty Wilde and the Wildcats with whom he was going to do a surprise guest spot the following night at the Tooting Granada. With Joe Brown flanking him as his first UK guitar player, he headed on to Manchester where he taped eleven songs with the house rhythm section, and the Vernons Girls singing back-up. That was the way Good organized *Boy Meets Girls*. When a major star was in town, he would tape all day, and then the performances would be aired as single song segments through the rest of the show's season.

Gene spent the rest of December touring France, Holland, Germany, and even had the shirt ripped off his back at a live TV show filmed at the prestigious Olympia in Paris. It wasn't until the new year, the first month (by some calculations) of the 1960s, that Gene finally headlined his first, twelve-date tour of the UK. (The compere was Don Arden. Later he would manage Vincent, but he's better known today as Ozzie Osbourne's father-in-law.) On that first tour, Gene had yet to integrate the Jack Good-inspired new look into the show, and still came on stage with his first backing band, Joe Brown with the Rockets, in his US stage clothes. The full leather outfit would not be seen live until the tour was extended for a further month, and Eddie Cochran was flown in to join the tour. It was only when Cochran was on the bill and providing Gene with a wildside sounding-board that Gene went to maximum-leather stage dramatics, as they renewed the symbiotic band-brothers relationship that would give rock and roll its first great might-have-been.

The accusation has been made more than once that what Jack Good's conceptualizing really did was to turn Gene Vincent into a comic book character, and, to a degree, this is

true. In the early days of rock, the medium
was definitely the message, and no one
thought too much about actually creating and
marketing a rock 'n' roll act as a planned
product. Elvis had his moves, Buddy Holly
had his glasses, years would pass before
Johnny Cash became the 'Man in Black', and
Little Richard was black, camp, and insane.
No more was needed. The first attempts at
overt star-making happened in England in the
mid-fifties, when Larry Parnes, the nation's
first big-time flamboyant rock promoter
attempted to cultivate and convert young
men – both with and without talent – into a
stable of homegrown rock idols to counter
the US originals who dominated record sales
in the formative phase of rock 'n' roll.
Parnes' first move was to endow each
potential star with a really stupid rock 'n' roll
name – Marty Wilde, Tommy Steele, Terry
Deane, Billy Fury, Duffy Power, Vince Eager,
Wee Willy Harris, Eden Kane, the list became
more daft as it grew longer. Some, like the
respected and ever-hip Georgie Fame would
remain saddled with their Parnes stable-

names for the rest of their careers. Parnes
operated according to a make-or-break
principle of stardom or oblivion, and sought
to achieve one-hit-wonders by any means
necessary, including strange outfits, padded-
out trousers, and weirdly colored haircuts.
Sometimes it worked, sometimes it didn't.
The recruited teenagers were infinitely
disposable, but the Parnes system was so
absurdly original that it would be parodied at
by punks some twenty years later, all he way
to the names and the coiffures, with Sid
Vicious at one Dadaist-suicide extreme, and
Billy Idol at the other with his blatant will-to-
triumph.

Jack Good's makeover of Gene, however
was something different. This was no attempt
to transform a callow youth into a household
sex-symbol. Good took the fully realized
sense of danger already generated by Gene to
a literal and visual extreme. Black leather,
hunched posture, gloves and totemic
medallion put it beyond question that Gene
was the demon bad-ass. He would hold the
title for the rest of his days, and, if anyone

doubts that the mutation was effective, they only need to look at Jim Morrison's invention of himself as the Lizard King, or how an almost identical process was used – omitting only the gloves and medallion – to bring Elvis Presley back to the hard edge of rock 'n' roll for his 1968 NBC TV comeback special. On the positive side, the Good makeover ensured that Gene would have a continuing career, and remain the Richard III of rock and roll until the end of his days. The darker outcome was that Gene was doomed to play only that character, with no time-off for good behaviour, if only because the character he had become wasn't in the good behaviour business.

The problem of the rock star being simultaneously being both an artist and a cartoon character, a creative force and a marketable product, has generated a lot of dilemmas down the years. In the initial struggle for fame, many performers have thrown themselves into a persona only to find out later that the strain can be crippling when persona and personality become one and the same. All too many of rock's superheroes have failed to provide themselves with a convenient alter-ego – a private Clarke Kent to the public Superman. Jim Morrison clearly had fatal problems keeping up with the extremes of the Lizard King. Arthur Brown is reputed to have, for a time, started to believe he was the God of Hellfire, while, on a somewhat more complex level, Syd Barrett had so much trouble living with his image of the withdrawn and romantic psychedelic poet that he finally withdrew altogether. Kurt Cobain took out a similar tortured junkie poet character with a shotgun. Jerry Garcia was about the most seemingly 'real' of musicians, but still required considerable doses of heroin to tolerate the 'reality.' Ozzie Osbourne went the reverse route in later life, when playing the fumbling, excess-damaged dad in the family's reality TV show, and erasing a prevalent public perception of Ozzie as a fully viable singer and songwriter. Perhaps the strangest piece of role playing – one that is highly relevant to the Gene Vincent story –

was that of Vince Taylor, an American expatriate working in France and blatant Vincent clone, who, after one minor hit, 'Long Black Cadillac', decided that he was Gene, and brought lawsuits claiming that Gene had stolen his act. Then, according to legend, Taylor took too much acid, changed into flowing white robes, and declared himself the new Messiah.

It really wasn't until the arrival of David Bowie and Ziggy Stardust that rock 'n' roll realized what you saw wasn't always what you got, and performers didn't have to maintain the illusion of their stage characters and their real life personalities being one and the same. Bowie was the first major star to dare the jump that has always alluded the likes of Prince and Michael Jackson. He discovered that he could assume characters like Ziggy or the Thin White Duke like costumes from the closet of his imagination, wear them while useful and then discard them – kill them off if need be – and move on to something else. It was a concept, however, that came too late for Gene

Vincent. He was never allowed go put down the persona of Richard III or the Screamin' End. Gene was in the rock 'n' role game too early to fully cope with what he was, what he had become, or what would be expected of him.

Billed by Larry Parnes as *The Anglo-American Beat Show*, the package featured Gene and Eddie Cochran as headliners, Billy Fury closed the first half, while Joe Brown, Georgie Fame, and Tony Sheridan were also featured on the bill. *The Anglo-American Beat Show*, although almost forgotten today, was in fact a major landmark in rock 'n' roll history. It was the UK's very first, all rock 'n' roll tour. Previously, even stars like Buddy Holly and Jerry Lee Lewis had been part of conventional variety shows, sandwiched between crooners, comedians, dancers, and dog acts.

All was well until the tour hit the notorious Glasgow Empire where audiences included members and followers of the infamous Glasgow gangs like The Young

Mental Shamrock, that had their roots in the fighting and feuding of Highland clans going back hundreds of years. The crowd at the Glasgow Empire never limited to itself to verbal disapproval of an act that it didn't like. Offending artistes would be driven from the stage in hail of beer bottles, and anything else that came to hand, and could actually be dragged from the stage by enraged, and usually fighting-drunk ticket holders, which put a literal twist on the desperate showbiz cry 'I'm dying out here!'

Joe Brown recalls, 'It was the worst gig we ever did. The crowds there were extremely rough. They generally threw bottles at the performers whether they disliked them or not. Glasgow Empire was known in the business as the 'Death Palace'. If you could go down in the Glasgow Empire, you could go down anywhere. But it was generally the sex-image types that got attacked, the pretty boy types. Poor old Billy Fury had a bad time. I was in the wings and could hear the whiskey bottles flying past. The girls loved him up there, but the boys took umbrage.

The band eventually deserted him and left him standing there. But Eddie Cochran went down good. And Gene did very well.'

Beneath the headline, 'Vincent, Cochran Rock Glasgow', the Glasgow Herald reported – 'Gene Vincent and Eddie Cochran descended on the Glasgow Empire on Monday with a frenzied swoop, evoking screams galore from the delighted fans. Judging by their reactions, the show will register strongly with admirers of Eddie Cochran's forceful singing act and Gene Vincent's leather-clad contortions-cum-singing. The pity was that both these artists words could hardly be heard against the instrumental backing and audience shouting. Through 'Hallelujah I Love Her So', Eddie built up to an earlier hit 'C'mon Everybody' and soon had customers in the beat mood. His only tactical error was in talking about being in England, resulting in cries of 'You're in Scotland!' Gene Vincent, on the other hand, is a more flamboyant showman, almost cuddling his microphone, kneeling and crawling on the stage, and generally leaping about like some leather-clad spaceman from another planet.'

On this extended UK tour, Vincent and Cochran would appear to have renewed and cemented the friendship that had flourished a year and half earlier in US. After the Glasgow date, Darlene Craddock, Gene's first wife, joined the tour for a couple of weeks. She remembers, 'Eddie was a very bubbly person. He was high-spirited and easy going. He was a nice guy and very good looking, but he knew it, though he didn't let it go to his head. Him and Gene would stay up half the night, playing their guitars and acting crazy', while Joe Brown is on record as observing. 'Eddie was like an older brother to Gene.'

With the advantage of hindsight, it's easy to identify the growing ties between Vincent and Cochran as having the potential of those symbiotic musical relationships of the Lennon/McCartney, Jagger/Richards, Jones/Strummer variety that would later prove the backbone and creative wellspring of truly great rock 'n' roll bands. Unfortunately, in 1958, and even in 1960, the world had yet to recognize this kind of male bonding for what it was, and the record business had no structure to accommodate it.

In the 1950s, the marketing moguls liked their teen idols, in every sense, single and separate. The only double acts they recognized were obvious duos like the Everly Brothers or Les Paul and Mary Ford. Bands invariably meant instrumental ensembles like The Ventures, and groups were vocal units like The Four Seasons or The Coasters. Maybe somewhere along the way, a bright innovator might have wondered if a rock 'n' roll band could be sold simultaneously as an homogeneous unit, *and* a collection of distinct individuals, like the Marx Brothers, the Three Stooges, or *The Magnificent Seven*. But they never did. The Shadows, both as independent recording artists and as Cliff Richard's very visible backing group, went part of the way, but it took the phenomenon of the raw Beatles to demonstrate that such a thing was possible. At first, though, even The Beatles were only seen as matching suits and moptops. It took time, and the advent of more sophisticated rock criticism, for both the world and the music business to recognize that the duo of Lennon-McCartney represented a driving force unlike anything that had existed before. Songwriting duos were nothing new, rock music had already accepted Leiber and Stoller, Goffin and King, Pomus and Schuman, but they had never been the performers. Lennon and McCartney were something wholly unique in rock 'n' roll.

It was one of those situations, however, that, once The Beatles had opened the door to this new mode of thinking, a creative tide of collaboration suddenly flowed through, either partners like Jagger and Richards, or solo composers like Brian Wilson or Pete Townshend writing specifically to the strengths of their bandmates. In a few short years, rock bands – who collectively shared not only the spotlight and the fan worship, but also the creative focus – would become the commercial bedrock of the entire pop industry. Being part of a band, one of a team, surrounded by the support of running buddies was also a refuge. John Lennon once admitted how in awe he always was of Elvis Presley, because Elvis was just one man taking on the adulation and projected fantasies of half the world. Lennon had seen the same worship and hysteria, but he'd always had the other three with him to share the stress and dissipate the pressure. To watch Presley struggling to cope with the insane superstar circus, without Paul, George, and Ringo, with whom Lennon had come up through the rough and tumble of Liverpool and Hamburg, never ceased the amaze the Beatle.

The fantasy that Gene and Eddie might have formed the world's first truly kickass rock 'n' roll band can be nothing more than pure speculation, but they certainly seemed to have what was required. Their personalities were exactly complimentary. Vincent was the consummate showman, the wildman who was always prepared to go the extra mile. Cochran was an innovator, a low budget recording wizard who could work wonders with the primitive studio equipment of the time. Although surviving film clips show Eddie Cochran as not altogether comfortable with the hip-swiveling, post-Elvis role into which he'd been cast, he certainly had the writing talent and the technical flair to counteract Vincent's highly erratic approach to making records, and his increasing inability to tell the good songs from the mediocre. Maybe, given time, the idea might have occurred to them without the example of The Beatles blazing the trail. Given more time, The Beatles might have shown Gene and Eddie the way to form the first supergroup headed by a pair of 'old school' 1950s rockers, but the one thing that Gene Vincent and Eddie Cochran didn't have was time. On April 17th, 1960, Cochran would die in an auto accident on a road outside Bristol, England.

It was a chauffeur-driven car and he hit a lamppost going about 80. Eddie went out the door... skidded 250 yards on the back of his head. I was thrown on the grass and had my whole left side broken up. I picked Eddie up and carried him. When we got to the hospital I told the doc: 'I'll give you a million dollars if you can save his life.' He said he was dying. I said 'He can't die.' He said, 'Well, he is.' I said 'He's not.' I guess I tried to help him too much. I had a doctor flown in by helicopter... a brain surgeon. He operated... then Eddie died. 272 concussions across the back of his head. I have a picture here (of Eddie Cochran), let me show you. This was made from a small picture I've got. I won't give it to nobody because it's mine. I treasure it as a treasured possession. Now see the crosses there? (Shows a photo of Cochran with several white cross-designs scattered above Cochran's head and in his hair.) *This was taken a day before he died. See, one of those crosses is right in his half... taken a day before he died. God... explain that! Can you explain the picture? Where'd the crosses come from? As far as I knew, they weren't there before. It's incredible.*

Gene Vincent, 1970

The death of Eddie Cochran was second blow to rock 'n' roll's early illusion of its own immortality.

Slightly more than a year earlier, on February 3rd, 1959, Buddy Holly, Ritchie Valens, and The Big Bopper had died in a plane crash. A chill of reality moved through the new music. Many individuals across the world who knew his music were touched by the death of Eddie Cochran, and his recordings were constantly repackaged and reissued from that time on.

The establishment of his legend as one of the primal figures in rock 'n' roll was greatly aided by the way in which he tended to record anything and everything in his home studio – demos, song ideas guitar and vocal effects – and left a massive from-the-vaults legacy.

No one, however, was effected by Cochran's death more than Gene. Joe Brown remembers: 'Eddie's death really shook Gene up. As far as I could tell, they were best friends. Rumour has it that Gene would have died too if he hadn't been so pissed. But he was so relaxed that he was just thrown around a little.'

On the fatal Sunday night, after completing a week at the Bristol Hippodrome, Gene and Eddie decided to rent a car to take them directly to Heathrow Airport, instead of taking a train, and having to make the complicated crosstown connections in central London. Riding with them was Cochran's girlfriend Sharon Sheeley. Gene was asleep – some, like Joe Brown, say passed out drunk – when the driver ran through the small town of Chippenham, Wiltshire, doing over seventy. It was there that he lost control of the car and spun into lamppost. Eddie was thrown against the roof, and then out of the door as the car was totalled. He died of head injuries a few hours later at St. Martin's Hospital in Bath. Gene was taken to the same hospital with a broken collarbone and broken ribs, and his leg was also damaged and had to be put in a new cast. He also seems to have had problems grasping exactly what had happened. 'I suppose I was in a daze, but I kept thinking the guy in the bed opposite mine was Eddie. Seeing him there gave me comfort. It was until I asked a visitor, "Why don't you go over and see how Eddie's getting on?" That's when I learned the truth.'

Gene was kept in the Bath hospital for three days and then discharged. He took a plane back to the US. Photos taken of him taken at Heathrow, a bent figure with a coat thrown over his shoulders, reveal a man in what looks to be a combination of shock and chronic depression. Surprisingly, though, he was back in the UK in less than two weeks to play a show at the Hanley Gaumont. Eddie Cochran's place on the bill was taken by Jerry Keller, a one-hit-wonder whose saccharine teen tune 'Here Comes Summer' had made the British charts. Although the audiences at the shows that extended on through May and June could see no outward difference in his performance, those around Gene noticed that he was withdrawn and hard to reach, and, from that point on, his personal and offstage life would grow progressively erratic. Ten years later, he would still be talking with an obsessive and sometimes near-deranged bitterness about Cochran's death.

Well, people aren't going to like this either, but… He had a girlfriend called Sharon Sheeley. She said she was engaged to him, which was the biggest goddamned lie I'd ever heard in my whole life. I never heard such a bunch of shit in my life. Anyway, we were in England on our way to London that night and Eddie said to me: 'Gene, instead of getting on the train and fightin' the whole way back, going with Sharon, why don't we just drive?' So we hired a car. Usually I got in first, then it was Eddie and her. But this one night, I don't know what happened, but she got in first, then Eddie and me. Eddie was killed cause he was in the middle. Now there's only one way he could have been killed. That was throwing himself across her body. It's the only way! We've tried to figure it out. Nobody's really told the truth! If she'd tell the truth for a change. That man was a good cat, man, and he's dead…You know, his mother and father never even called me. Never even talked to me. But that man was like my brother. I knew him like nobody else did. They have never even called! Eddie told me things, whispering before he died, that he wanted to tell them. Have they called and asked me? No... I'd gladly tell them. Why don't they ask me?... I'll tell you why they don't. We had a man... we were working almost eight months on the road. We had a man called Riley. Now we had picked up almost a quarter of a million dollars on our tours... me and Eddie... and we were leaving for Bristol that night. And Riley he... now, how do you go about stealing quarter of a million dollars? Can I tell you how? He booked himself into a mental hospital, got out and collected the money and booked himself back in. Now you can't touch him. Who are you going to get? The police?

Gene Vincent 1970

Chapter Four

WHEN I HEARD in the late autumn of 1969 that Gene Vincent would be playing the Country Club in Hampstead, backed by Brit rock revivalists the Wild Angels, I couldn't decide whether I was excited or dismayed. I already knew that he was in failing health and pretty much on the skids. If I went along to the show I suspected that I would be seeing one of my personal legends for the last time. I knew I'd be watching a man at the end of a long decline. For more than fifteen years, even before he had an international hit with 'Be-

Bop-A-Lula', Gene had been living a regime so profoundly destructive it was a near-miracle he had even made it to the end of the 1960s, let alone to be attempting yet another European tour. The tour itself spoke volumes of how far the mighty had fallen. The Country Club was a joint that held maybe four hundred max, a ramshackle building in back of a parking lot, down an alley beside Belsize Park underground station. Hell, I had played there with the Deviants more times than I cared to remember, and the booking was a clear indication of the humiliating depths to which the 'rock 'n' roll Richard III' had sunk. When Gene came on he was trying hard, holding the old pose, but his voice was painfully weak as though worn threadbare from an endless diabolic conflict. His face was pale and puffy and he had put on the kind of unhealthy weight characteristic of heavy drinkers. Although I didn't know it at the time, the problems created by his injured and constantly patched-up leg were just as out of control as his career and lifestyle. Osteomyelitis had set in, and every doctor he saw who saw him, and wrote the inevitable prescription for painkillers also warned him that amputation was only a matter of time.

Of course, I wanted to see the man, whatever condition he might be in, as did many others. The place was packed, but as I looked around at the applauding crowd at the end of Gene's short, barely twenty-minute set, I knew that we were all engaged in a form of mass denial and were stamping and cheering for something that hardly existed any more. Maybe we were clapping and hollering for our own lost youth. There was no encore. Gene only came back to the stage to acknowledge the standing ovation with a weary curtain call, and I think I knew I would never see him again. In a previous book, *Give The Anarchist A Cigarette*, I wrote how the Blackfoot Tribe have a proverb that goes 'When legends die, there are no more dreams, and when there are no more dreams, there is no more greatness.' I knew, that night at the Country Club, that I was watching the death of a legend, and, if not a death, certainly a diminishment of greatness. I wasn't aware, however, that death was more than just a metaphor for the fall of Gene as a showman. Death – the real grim reaper death – was already moving in his direction. He had a scant two years to live. On October 21st, 1971, at the age of thirty six, Gene Vincent would die, after a life in which he experienced more, both good and bad, high and low, sublime and ridiculous, than many men twice his age.

The legend of Gene Vincent has always made the claim that the two great setbacks in his life were the pre-fame motorcycle accident that ruined his leg, and the death of Eddie Cochran. For the most part, the facts would seem to agree. That his leg was the cause of pain and problems for most of his adult life goes without saying, and Cochran's death is an observable watershed in both Gene's career and his private life. Whether the latter was the whole story, as the legend would lead us to believe, is debatable. Paul Peek and other members of the Blue Caps, and even Little Richard talk about how Gene could be a mean and even dangerous drunk back when Eddie Cochran was still very much alive and kicking. Tales of his drinking, drugs, debauchery, and fondness for firearms go well back into the 1950s. On the other hand, prior to 1960, Vincent seemed to have the ability to recover from his lapses, but after that disastrous year, madness came a lot closer to turning into a way of life.

Although the details conflict, Gene would appear to have had some kind of breakdown in the months after Eddie Cochran died. In June 1960, he had a hit in Britain, France, and Germany with a reworking of the old Al Dexter country classic 'Pistol Packin' Mama'. The Eddie Cochran arrangement of the tune had been cut with Georgie Fame and the Beat Boys in EMI's St. John's Wood studio almost as soon as Gene was released from hospital, and it reached number sixteen in the UK charts, eerily juxtapostitioned against Eddie's 'Three Steps To Heaven' at number three. The Cochran single, with its maudlin, and quasi prophetic title had been blatantly rush-released by Liberty/United Artists to cash in on the singer's death, but hasn't that always been the way of it in rock 'n' roll? Gene meanwhile was on a seemingly endless British tour promoting his single, but, sometime in the same month 'Pistol Packin' Mama' was released, he clearly snapped. The imaginary death of his daughter Melody was used as an excuse to duck out of his contracts, and he abruptly flew back to where his first wife Darlene was living in Portland, Oregon, and stayed there through the rest of the summer and early fall, doing a few local shows but mainly resting. For once, Gene Vincent was at least making moves to take a little care of himself. Darlene Craddock, who gave birth to their son, Gene Jr in October of 1960, even claims that Gene was talking about quitting performing and becoming a disc jockey, but the tale would seem to be one of dubious credence. Gene might have said it during his time off the road in order to keep his wife happy, or at least quiet, but the statement is contradicted by the rest of his life, that totally added up to relentless demonstration of how, whatever else might happen, Gene

was absolutely incapable of giving up live
rock 'n' roll.

Once Gene Jr was born, Vincent's need for
an audience very quickly began dragging him
back to the craziness of the road. The only
minor mitigation was that he held the wild
demons at bay long enough at least to start
slowly. He did some tentative tryout shows in
the Pacific north west, and then took a
working break, heading down to Los Angeles
to cut new tracks at the Capitol Tower in
Hollywood. Unfortunately, the outcome of
the sessions was a clutch of infinitely
forgettable schmalz; string-smothered pop
tunes that were plainly going nowhere. With
no immediate chance of rebuilding his career
in the US, he had little choice but to accept a
management offer from Don Arden and head
back to Europe, where he at least had an
obsessive and adoring public who were
prepared to forgive and even admire his
excesses.

Through 1961, Gene shuttled between
Britain and America. The European end of
things went well. The single 'She She Little

Sheila' made the UK charts and stayed there for eleven weeks. He cut the highly superior, 'I'm Going Home' at Abbey Road, and that too charted. Back in the USA, though, he couldn't catch a break. He filmed a couple of musical numbers for a dire remake of the movie *State Fair*, that starred Pat Boone and Connie Francis, only to have his segment cut from the final print. He returned to Niles, California, the Bay Area town outside of San Francisco where Darlene had relocated with the kids, only to find that she had taken off. She would explain: 'I had just had enough. I wanted a real marriage. I wanted to settle down. I just hated life on the road. I thought it was nuts. But Gene thought I was nuts. I wanted to break off with him, but I was scared. He still had all those pistols and knives.'

Back in England, he participated in another god awful film, *It's Trad, Dad*, in which he performed the song 'Spaceship To Mars' with Sounds Incorporated, but due to a lack of initiative on the part of Capitol Records, the tune wasn't released as a simultaneous single, and no hit was forthcoming from the experience. In July of 1962, following a highly successful tour with Brenda Lee on which the pair were billed as the 'King and Queen of Rock', Gene was teamed with producer Bob Barrett to cut 'King of Fools' and a twist-tempo reworking of 'Be-Bop-A-Lula', but this release also failed to make a dent, this time round ostensibly because a bureaucratic work permit foul-up prevented him from touring the UK to promote it.

Although it seemed at the time that Gene was failing by a combination of bad timing, bad luck and mishandled details, a much larger and inescapable truth lurked beneath everything. The entire face, focus, and attitude of rock was diametrically changing. As Gene lurched from 'Spaceship to Mars' to 'King of Fools', The Beatles were writing and recording 'Please Please Me', 'Love Me Do', and 'She Loves You'. They would rapidly be followed by the Rolling Stones, Bob Dylan, The Animals, and the rest of the conquering army of 1960s rock 'n' roll.

Maybe with the inventive mind of Eddie Cochran to help him, he could have been one of the few, like Johnny Cash and Roy Orbison, who made an at least marginally comfortable transition from the first rock 'n' roll decade to the second, and maintained a recording career in the face of a musical revolution. On his own, however, Gene seemed incapable of coming up with appropriate material for the new generation of record buyers. While Johnny Kidd, his chief rival in the leather and sideburns business could cut contemporary sounding hits like 'Shaking All Over' and 'I'll Never Get Over You', and even Vince Taylor, the Parisian pretender could come up with 'Brand New Cadillac', Gene floundered in the studio turning out grotesqueries like 'Lavender Blue'.

Which was unfortunate because, in a lot of respects, Gene was better positioned than most to handle the coming of The Beatles and all that followed. John Lennon and Paul McCartney were devoted fans. He had met the Liverpool boys in Hamburg, and seen them play at the Star Club. They had even opened for him at the Cavern in Liverpool, although it's moot whether Gene remembered that with any clarity. John Lennon particularly admired Gene, who was a major influence, right down to The Beatles ' Hamburg-era leather suits. A story circulated that, one night, The Beatles had actually backed him when his own band failed to show because of car trouble, but this may be totally fanciful. Closer to the truth was that, somewhere along the line, Gene had spotted the band's potential, and even entertained ideas – if only in his own addled imagination – of somehow managing them, although that reality scarcely bears thinking about.

Over and above his Beatles connection, though, what Gene really had going for him was the power of his live performances. His black leather act had been so extreme that it had elevated him from the fate of most rockabilly zoot-suit cowboys. Since he seemed to be from a dark quadrant of outer space already, he wasn't so completely tied to a specific time and genre. His live talent, however, was also a double edged sword. To play live, he had to tour, and once on tour, he had proved, over and over again, that he was wholly incapable of easing back on the overindulgence and keeping from decimating himself.

Before I went to England in 1960, I played in Europe. I went to Hamburg and met a group there. I was very impressed with them. We met and talked a lot... that was at the Star Club... They were really good. Now they're called John Lennon and The Beatles. They didn't have a record out or nothing. God, I could have picked them up so cheaply... which was so foolish of me. But, like I said, I'm a singer, not a bloody business man.

Gene Vincent 1970

Gene Vincent entered a realm that has become the fate of too many musicians with live followings but failing recording careers. He found himself in the Flying Dutchman twilight zone of perpetual touring, and the attendant perpetual unreality. He hardly enjoyed any permanent home, and his days – or, more accurately, his nights – were passed in haze of trains, planes, cars, and hotels, made even less distinguishable from one another by booze and painkillers. Gene generated a lot of cash on the road, but precious little of it found its way into any permanent bank account of his own. When the business was done, the accounts reckoned, the band had been paid, and the damages compensated, so little was left that the only real option was to re-up for another tour of duty.

Gene became a permanent fixture on a European concert circuit that was being simultaneously criss-crossed by Bo Diddley, a recovering Jerry Lee Lewis, Fats Domino, Little Richard, when he didn't have religion, as well as home-grown product like Billy Fury, Marty Wilde, Cliff and the Shads, and Johnny Halliday. On paper, Gene should have been doing okay, but all reports indicate that every tour hemorrhaged money, as tour managers, crew, and a succession of wives and girlfriends kept the change, and went through his wallet.

It might have helped some if Gene hadn't been quite so drunk. He might have saved his ass had he been just slightly in control of his own destiny, but that wasn't the way of it with Gene. He was the wild man of old time rock 'n' roll, and was never been capable of faking it. By 1962, he was an alcoholic of notable proportions even by the lax standards of the rock world. A epic history of drunken outrage steadily built as Gene lurched from drunken rages to comatose non-communication. Alan Holmes, one of the horn section in Sounds Incorporated remembers Gene as being 'a bit of a schizo. He had an on-stage personality and an offstage personality. When he was sober, he was a really nice guy. It was like he was waiting in the wings sniffing Jekyll and Hyde powder.' Tour manager Henry Henroid tells a similar story. 'I'd say Gene was schizophrenic. He could be so kind and yet so hateful. You had to be very strong with Gene. There was no other way. You loved him one minute and hated him the next.' The love and hate was pushed to extremes, even for Gene, in 1962 while he was having an affair with – and subsequently married to – a dancer called Margie Russell, whom he insisted on taking on the road with him. Margie, it seemed, had been a familiar face and body around the early London rock scene, and the knowledge, and constant backstage reminders that she so obviously had enjoyed intimate friendships with a lot of musicians could drive Gene to violent bouts of drunken jealously. Once triggered, he would rage at various members of his entourage that they'd been sleeping with Margie behind his back. Later, after Gene's death, Margie Russell would sell her story to the British tabloids, in which she referred to Geneas a 'tempestuous rock singer and marathon drinker.'

At regular intervals managers and minders tried to 'be strong with Gene' and keep him off the booze. Unfortunately Gene was well practiced in the art of a drunk's deception, and he'd thwart their efforts by sneaking off to bars, stashing bottles in tour buses and hotel rooms, and, when those trying to protect him grew wise to these dodges, he would resort to hiding miniatures in the cast on his leg. Henry Henroid recalls: 'Gene was very clever. I swear he could smell bars. In the middle of the night he could find them.'

The problem was further compounded by Gene's obsession with firearms. In the US, where the right to bear arms is constitutionally guaranteed, nobody thought too much about a rock singer from East Virginia, no matter how drunk, travelling with a couple of pistols in his luggage, but, in Europe, the picture was very different. Gene was constantly crossing borders, moving from country to country, each with a different level of gun control. All travelling rock bands quickly learn the idiosyncracies of local law. How, for example, you can freely buy switchblades and spring-loaded blackjacks in Paris, but that the same items are seriously illegal if one attempts to take them back to London. Gene seemed to run the gamut of whatever weapons he could get his hands on.

In England, he found he could buy powerful target air pistols right over the counter in toy shops and sports equipment stores, and these, for a while, became a craze. In Germany, he discovered that teargas guns were readily available, and, as a result, nearly asphyxiated himself in a Hamburg hotel room, and came close to being arrested when he fired one in the Star Club. Gene also didn't care if the weapons he acquired with such unpleasant schoolboy glee were legal or not. As Alan Holmes notes, 'He always appealed to hard men and would-be bruisers', and all too many petty criminals in Gene's European fan following gained an audience with the star by offering to sell him a piece.

The final factor in the gathering madness was, of course, the deteriorating condition of Gene's leg. For years, it had never been allowed to heal. His rock 'n' roll career had taken off while he was still an out-patient at the Naval hospital in Norfolk, and he hadn't let the fact that the shattered bones had never properly set stand in the way of fame and fortune. From 1956 onwards, medical treatment was rarely more than a rough patch job, and a prescription of antibiotics and painkillers. During the better periods he could manage to get around with just a steel leg brace, but in the bad times, the leg would be in a cast and Gene would be hobbling on crutches. One of the unfortunate side effects of a constant diet of pain pills was that Gene never really knew when he was hurting himself. He refused ever to compromise and back off from the wild physicality of his performances, but the stage proved to the fatal combat zone where damage was constantly being done. A cast would crack, a bone fragment would be dislodged, but, at the time Gene would be too numbed to notice. All too often, he would only become blearily aware of the problem hours later when his leg started to swell or other symptoms manifested themselves. This would galvanize the road crew into a panic hunt for a doctor or emergency room in a strange town. Every so often, Gene would encounter a doctor who would throw up his hands in horror, and declare that any further treatment was hopeless, osteomyelitis was inevitable, and the leg should come off. Gene resisted any such suggestion but he must have walked around with the nagging certainty that, sooner or later, he would lose his leg.

That Gene would – one way or the other – crash and burn was also inevitable. The only real question was where and when. As it turned out, it would be the autumn of 1965, when the London evening tabloids ran banner headlines 'POP STAR IN HOTEL GUN OUTRAGE'. The exact details have largely been covered up and glossed over, but it would appear that, with the estranged Margie Russell hustling him from one side, and money problems with his manager, the notorious Don Arden, on the other, Gene finally snapped. In a hotel in London's Lancaster Gate, Gene went nuts with an air-pistol and attempted to hi-jack an elevator full of guests. How the incident was actually resolved, or whether Gene was formally arrested and charged, are conclusions lost in the mists of time. The only solid information is that he abruptly left the UK, and did not return for another four years. Maybe a deal was cut, or maybe he simply jumped whatever bail had been set, and took it on the lam. Whatever the inside story, Gene Vincent's reign as the rock 'n' roll Richard III was finally over.

Don't talk to me about managers. I don't have a manager any more. Up until a few months ago I had a manager who I trusted – and managers need trusting – but right now this guy's got $28,000 of my money and I can't touch him.

Gene Vincent 1965

The doctors want to take my leg off, but I keep saying no. The way medicine progresses every single day, they might find something to cure it, and I'm not willing to take the risk. I have to take morphine to kill the pain when it really gets bad, and the last time I came to England I got really whacked out. My leg is giving me a little problem all right, but I try not to let it beat me.

Gene Vincent 1970

That Gene Vincent and Jim Morrison of The Doors should meet and even strike up a bar-buddy relationship was almost too perfect to be true. Morrison owed so much to Gene, and, in rock 'n' roll, that kind of karmic debt is very rarely paid. That it should be in this instance is an extreme and delightful rarity. If anyone was Gene Vincent's cosmic and spiritual son, it had to be Jim Morrison.

From his leather suits to his stage posture of clinging to the mike stand, sometimes as much for dear life as his mentor, Morrison had taken it all from Gene, and then expanded and transcended. Where Gene had always dealt in simple pop tunes, The Doors had elaborate and poetic lyrics, and songs that could, in some cases, meander through a number of different movements. Where Gene had originated the leather monster look, Morrison had defined and romanticized it. He was the Lizard King, he could do anything. Morrison invented a quasi-mystic anagram of his own name – Mr Mojo Rising. Gene had never invented an anagram in his entire life. Jim quoted

Nietzsche, while Gene quoted comic books. Where Gene Vincent's rock 'n' roll world was close to illiterate, peopled with nothing more than easily sketched comic book characters, Jim Morrison had created a darkly detailed, almost operatic landscape of shamanism and violence, feral children, monsters and princesses, fires in the hills, and blood in the streets.

Both men, however, were in helplessly in tune with the times that shaped them, and both men also drank to excess to dull the noise in their heads. It wouldn't be the first time the single fact of a shared booze habit has been the basis for a friendship. Jim and Gene started to meet regularly at a shot and beer joint called the Shamrock at the Silver Lake end of Santa Monica Boulevard, that would, ironically, a decade on, at the end of the 1970s, become a watering hole for the LA punks and garage bands.

At exactly the same time, British DJ John Peel, along with Clive Selwood, the then boss of Elektra Records UK, formed the Dandelion label. Peel, who had made his name on the pirate radio ship Radio London and then moved to the BBC's newly-established Radio One, was known at the time as the radio epicentre of all things hippie, and was primarily judged by his patronage of Marc Bolan and support for bands like Fairport Convention and Family.

Many of his listeners weren't aware that Peel was also a rocker from way back, and a total Gene admirer. When some sub-standard Vincent tapes came to him, via arch Vincent fan Adrian Owlett, they started Peel thinking, and the outcome of these thoughts was the idea that Dandelion should put Gene in a studio to cut an album. Whether Peel instinctively sensed that Gene was already three parts into the twilight zone, and it might be a last chance to get him on vinyl is open to debate, but the combination of his relationship with Morrison, and Peel's determination to at least get one more recording out of the man, seemed to have initiated a Save Gene Vincent movement.

Saving Gene, however, was not a totally altruistic act. By 1969, a back-to-roots movement was becoming noticeable in rock 'n' roll. Sections of the rock audience where beginning to overdose on the more grandiose excesses of psychedelic music and, worse still, it's supposedly drug-free and over elaborate fellow traveler, 'progressive rock'. Bob Dylan, after a long and supposedly medical hiatus had released the almost country sounding *John Wesley Harding*, and The Band had started a small revolution with the complex, but still magnificently earthbound, *Music From Big Pink*. Previously acid-dosed rockers were coming up for air and digging out their Eddie Cochran records for a dose of simplicity. Not least of these was Pete Townshend. The Who had started featuring 'Summertime Blues' in their set as a easy counterbalance to the creative marathon of *Tommy*. Elvis had performed the live rock 'n' roll portions of his NBC comeback special in a black leather suit, and folks on both sides of the Atlantic seemed to be hankering for the old time, straight-ahead rock of a dozen years earlier. In the USA, one manifestation of the post-flower-power, retro-craze was the fifties revival revue, Sha-Na-Na, which was billed at psychedelic ballrooms alongside Quicksilver Messenger Service and The Grateful Dead, and ultimately playing at Woodstock. In the UK, the Wild Angels, who would back Gene on his penultimate British tour, were enjoying a similar domestic vogue. The term 'rock revival' was being heard. Giant package shows were being promoted at which a new generation was able to see live performances by Jerry Lee Lewis, Bo Diddley, Little Richard, and Bill Haley and the Comets for themselves. Gene would headline at one of the these events at New York's Felt Forum, the smaller auditorium at Madison Square Garden, and he would also play at San Francisco's original hippie Mecca, the Avalon Ballroom, double billed with Commander Cody and his Lost Planet Airmen. All this does not minimize the leap of faith that everyone connected with project that would create the album *I'm Back And I'm Proud* was making, but it does show that the saving of Gene Vincent had at least a minimum of commercial logic behind it.

Unfortunately, like everything connected with Gene, the rescue operation didn't go smoothly. The first problem was the choice of Kim Fowley as producer. Fowley had been a fixture around the Los Angeles music scene since the time of Phil Spector. At some six feet four inches tall and with crazy eyes, Fowley tended to resemble a towering Frankenstein's monster in mod threads, who always had a hustle going. He had brought the world 'Alley Oop' by the Hollywood Argyles, 'Surfing Bird' by the Trashmen, and would go on to instigate the Runaways. He alternately collaborated and fell out with Frank Zappa, but never seemed to quite make it to the A-list star status he so clearly craved. Any way you sliced it, the sessions were set to be strange. But with luminaries like Johnny Meeks on guitar, Skip Battin from the Byrds on bass, and Red Rhodes on pedal steel, the Dandelion sessions seemed set, in theory, to be a winner. They even acquired the status of an LA underground event, frequented by Jim Morrison and assorted Doors plus hangers on, who watched while the musicians did the best they could – particularly Gene who, even in a context where everyone else seemed to be drinking, had sworn off the booze for the duration. Even without alcohol, however, Fowley and Gene smashed egos, and Gene would make late-night phone calls to all and sundry, complaining about Fowley, 'They've sent a madman over here.' Skip Battin recalls: 'Gene was a perfectionist and Fowley liked to move pretty quickly. Gene tried very hard, but he was pretty sick at the time. His leg was bothering him and he was in constant pain.' Johnny Meeks is less charitable. 'They (Vincent and Fowley) slaughtered that damned album.' Slaughtered or not, *I'm Back And I'm Proud* wasn't without its moments, most particularly a fine reading of JP Richardson's 'White Lightning' with a sound not unlike that of The Band, and a good, but maybe ill-considered, 'Be-Bop-A-Lula '69', plus a workmanlike 'Rockin' Robin' and an epic 'In The Pines', a traditional lament from the same folk-song root as the better known 'House Of The Rising Sun.'

I'm Back And I'm Proud was released to mixed reviews. One of the most favorable was by Simon Frith in *Rolling Stone*, who went further than just the new offering, reminding the world just what an innovator Gene had been in his prime. 'Gene Vincent's music was tough and very edgy, and his best records were extraordinarily tense. The excitement of 'Be-Bop-A-Lula' comes less from the beat than the feeling of suppressed energy, and the feeling that Vincent and the Blue Caps are holding themselves back. Gene Vincent had one of the most remarkable voices of the 1950s, with great range and perfect control, but it always had a neurotic feel, slightly anxious. He used his voice as an instrument, and the sound of his voice was always more important than the words in giving his songs atmosphere. The tension was a result of the conflict between Vincent's originality and the demands of a rock 'n' roll single. The Blue Caps added to this tension. Both Cliff Gallup and Johnny Meeks had an extraordinary ability to play all the instrumental-break cliches while still sounding original. On 'Blue Jean Bop', for example, Gallup sounds as though at any moment he might break out and destroy the record altogether.' In the end, though, Frith compared *I'm Back And I'm Proud* with the 1950s recordings and decided sadly that: 'No one makes records like that any more, not even Gene Vincent'.

Do I seem mad at all to you? I can't explain it, but I do notice that when anything like this is said, I'm not around to hear it. I guess they wouldn't dare say it if I was.
Gene Vincent 1965

Haven't you heard? I've only got a year to live. The leg's got cancer.
Gene Vincent 1969

In the film of Gene Vincent's life, the *Rock & Roll Revival Festival* at Varsity Stadium in Toronto, Canada, should have been the final triumphant moment, the redemption at the end of the third act. Unfortunately life is never quite as idealized as the movies. The 1969 festival in Toronto has been immortalized in rock 'n' roll legend as the one and only appearance of John Lennon and the Plastic Ono Band, and location for recording of *Live Peace In Toronto*. Although the event is recognized as a landmark – maybe the final landmark – by diehard Gene Vincent fans, his presence on the bill was somewhat overshadowed by the ex-Beatle's publicity machine. That Gene should appear on the show was largely instigated by Jim Morrison, either while he and Gene were drinking at the Shamrock or during the course of the *I'm Back And I'm Proud* sessions. In the first enthusiasm of the moment, everyone agreed that that Gene should appear with The Doors. It was a magnificent idea, but when it was learned that The Doors would have to show up early at the festival to accommodate Gene, things were rapidly scaled down. Gene would play instead with Alice Cooper's band, and, indeed, their pre-metal guitar rock was actually better suited to his style than Ray

Manzarek's always too nightclub-sounding keyboards. When Gene did come out, noticeably overweight, but wearing his black leather jacket, the vast crowd drawn by Lennon and The Doors seemed to sense that a page of history was being turned. At the end of an emotional 'Be-Bop-A-Lula', Lennon came on stage and embraced a weeping Gene.

Oh that it might have all ended there. But, as repeatedly observed, nothing in the life of Gene Vincent was ever that tidy or painless. The triumph in Toronto, and *I'm Back And I'm Proud* not withstanding, Gene was broke and needed to work, and the most obvious solution was yet another quicky tour of France and the UK to promote the album and earn some fast cash. Gene returned briefly to Los Angeles after Toronto, but, within a matter of days, he was on a plane to London. The Heathrow-bound flight turned out to be an ill omen of what was to come. Gene became loudly drunk, and Tom Jones – a Vincent fan from way back and also on the plane – was forced to step in and smooth things out. The French leg of the tour proved a disaster, with dubious promoters absconding with money, equipment, and even some of Gene's clothes. The UK dates started with equal chaos, as former manager Don Arden apparently attempted to exact organizational revenge on Gene – for supposed breach of their management contract – by sending heavies to exact payment in kind from some of the earlier shows, but this harassment ceased as Gene moved closer to the bookings in London, and was accompanied by a BBC camera crew shooting a documentary. The show at the Country Club that I attended, and then others at the chic Speakeasy and the London Palladium, also backed by the Wild Angels, made Gene too high-profile for anyone, Arden included, to cause him problems.

At the Speakeasy – London's musicians-and-groupies premier after-hours joint – John Lennon, George Harrison, Keith Moon, Pete Townshend, and Jeff Beck all turned out to see Gene, and Georgie Fame – a veteran of playing keyboards behind Gene from the days of the Beat Boys. This power jolt of respect, acclaim, and attention, from a cross section of British rock luminaries, energized Gene, and he gave a stunning and powerful performance. An energy boost on a different level also occurred at the London Palladium. This time, it was the old-time British Teddy Boys who raised Gene to a level of performance through which these arch rock 'n' roll conservatives could – for a half hour or so – recapture their lost youth. At the legendary London variety theatre, which had seen shows by Charlie Chaplin, Judy Garland, Marlene Dietrich, Frank Sinatra, The Beatles and the Rolling Stones, the Teds took Gene as high as he could ever have hoped. In drape jackets, drain-pipe pants, and thick crepe-soled brothel creepers, they had started by viciously booing the supporting acts, the Impalas and the Nashville Teens, but then turned around, howled and danced in the aisles, when Vincent took the stage, just like it was 1959, okay?

Again it was a case of had-it-all-ended-right-there, had Gene left the stage at the

Palladium and simply hung it up for a couple of years, regained his health, and then returned as a country singer, maybe the world's musical romance with Gene the Rocker might have closed with some kind of happy ending. The reality was that Gene had really no option but to keep dragging out an increasingly evident final curtain. From London, he returned to Los Angeles, and for a moment, he seemed to be pulling things together. Tom Ayres, an old acquaintance from the 1950s, who had toured on the same bill with Gene more than once, playing with the Johnny Burnette trio, became Gene's manager. Initially Ayres seems to have had the same motivation as John Peel and Jim Morrison – that somehow Gene had to be diverted from his current and incredibly self-destructive path, essentially to save his life. Ayres told author Brit Hagarty, for *The Day The World Turned Blue*: 'The whole pace of rock 'n' roll was killing Gene. We wanted to slide him into a sort of Jerry Lee Lewis semi-country style. I wanted Gene to maintain his own permanent band so we could maintain him. We realized that Gene couldn't continue on the way he was doing.'

Ayres also managed the Sir Douglas Quintet and he sold the idea to Neil Bogart at Casablanca Records that Gene and the quintet should cut an album together for Bogart's Karma Sutra subsidiary. The Dandelion deal had been a one off, and so in the spring of 1970, Gene and the Sir Douglas Quintet – minus Doug Sahm – when into the Sound Factory in Los Angeles, and cut some of the most god-awful tracks that Gene had ever committed to tape. Released as *If Only You Could See Me Now*, the record was supposedly an attempt to put Gene into a contemporary, early-seventies context. This had been attempted with a degree of success on a couple of cuts like 'White Lightning' on *I'm Back And I'm Proud*, but on *If Only You Could See Me Now* the effort was severely hampered by the fact that the 'modernizing' of Gene was attempted by utilizing the most unpleasant excesses of what was then considered 'modern'. His vocals were punctuated by detrimentally ugly fuzz/wah-

wah guitar tedium, and tracks like 'Slow
Times Coming' and 'Tush Hog' timed out at
over nine and seven uninspired minutes
respectively.

Through 1970 and the beginning of 1971,
Gene, with the help of Ayres, seemed to
remain in a holding pattern. Neither *If Only
You Could See Me Now*, nor it's follow-up
The Day The World Turned Blue (the same
title used for Bret Hagarty's biography) set
any worlds on fire, and Gene turned back to
live performances for pure survival. He
shuttled in and out of LA playing, clubs,
ballrooms, rock revival shows. Although he
had curtailed his drinking for a while after
signing with Tom Ayres, Gene was back on
the bottle and, in their resumed binges at the
Shamrock, Gene exhibited bouts of behavior
that even Jim Morrison – the man who
would dangle by one hand from 20th floor
hotel balconies – declared crazy. He did
another tour of France and England that,
although some shows are remembered as
exceptional, like the one at London's
Fishmongers' Arms, was as big a mess as the

previous excursion. Gene's final marriage to the petit Jackie Frisco had broken up after six years, and he was now travelling with a singer called Marcia Avron – who one friend described tersely as 'flashy looking with lots of makeup'. It seems to have been at Avron's urging that Gene cut two tracks for B&C Records with the Brit rock-a-billy combo, the Houseshakers. The only motivation for lackluster retreads of 'Say Mama' and 'I'm Movin' On' could have been quick cash, because, in so doing Gene breached, and ultimately terminated, his deal with Casablanca, and placed himself well on the wrong side of Bogart and Ayres.

By mid 1971, the holding pattern had turned into a headlong plunge. Following the break up with Frisco, and his contractual falling out with Neil Bogart and Tom Ayres, Gene hit the bottle big time. The vultures had been circling over the last UK tour. Margaret Russell had him briefly arrested for non-payment of child support, Don Arden's heavies dogged his heels, as did writs from British Inland Revenue, but now the scavengers seemed to be closing in, anticipating a corpse. He continued to work, but reports of Gene on the road were becoming tales of terminal desperation. Finally, in September of that year, he accepted yet another UK tour, although, in hindsight, the idea should have seemed close to suicidal. Ultra-loyal fan Adrian Owlett talks of seeing Gene close to the end of this absurd series of dates. 'His reason was completely gone. He was talking complete gibberish. He was incredibly paranoid. I just looked at this man sitting on the bed with head in his hands, and he was utterly depressed and suicidal.'

Gene made it back to LA only to find Marcia Avron had taken a maliciously flashy powder with his furniture and whatever was left in the joint bank account that Gene had set up against the advice of most of his remaining friends. She had even taken his stereo. Gene promptly went on an intensive drunk, finally destroying the already ulcerated lining of his stomach. Sometime in the first forty-eight hours after his return to LA, Jackie Frisco must have made contact with him because she angrily called his mother, Louise Craddock, who now lived in trailer home in the LA suburb of Saugus. 'I know Gene's dying. I saw it on my father's face and I saw it on Gene's. And I don't want any part of it.'

Alarmed, Craddock drove to Gene's stripped home in Simi Valley and insisted that he come home with her. Efforts to persuade him to check into a hospital failed, so she compromised and took him back to Saugus where she hoped she could look after him herself. Soon after stumbling into his mother's home, weak but raving, Gene apparently fell to his knees and said: 'Mama, if I get through this, I'm going to be a better man.' Then he began vomiting blood. Finally he looked up at his mother. 'Mama, you can phone the ambulance now.' The ambulance came, but, within the hour, he was dead.

But even death didn't go smoothly for poor Gene Vincent. Jackie Frisco, having changed her mind about wanting no part of it, by all accounts turned the funeral into an hysterical circus, demanding that the coffin be reopened to see that it was really Gene inside, and repeatedly insisting that he should have a military funeral paid for by the Veteran's Administration. Meanwhile, his sister Donna had recently fallen under the thrall of con artist and guru Tony Alamo, a one-time garment-district hustler from New York's 7th Avenue who, in the name of God, tended to divest the faithful of their savings, and then set them to work in slave-labour sweatshops manufacturing rhinestone cowboy clothes for the likes of Glen Campbell and Dolly Parton. Cult predators descended on Gene's few remaining possessions, carrying off guitars, memorabilia and stage outfits. Even the flowers that had been sent by fans all over the world were intercepted and stolen. Johnny Meeks sums up the irony of it all. 'It was crazy. I thought, 'Man, typical Gene. He can't even die right. There's always gotta be some kinda problem.'

Buried in a leather jacket and a blue shirt, the mortal remains of Gene lie beneath an ugly headstone in the Eternal Valley Memorial Home, close beside the San Fernando Highway. The inscription reads:

IN LOVING MEMORY OF HUSBAND,
SON, AND FATHER VINCENT EUGENE
CRADDOCK known as GENE VINCENT
recording star.
FEB11, 1935-OCT 12 1971.'

After he died, he had the sweetest smile on his face. He wanted to die. He was glad to think he was getting out of this mess he was in.

Louise Craddock

Chapter Five

GENE VINCENT WAS a drunk, a pillhead and, at times, a dangerous and creatively erratic asshole, but that may have been the true power of the man. If rock was literature, he'd probably have been Jean Genet. He was the true pioneer of rock 'n' roll self-destruction in the grand manner. He made it clear, from first to last, that the music he played was about the dark side and the underbelly, and he conducted his career as though that music was some kind of mortal combat with destiny. His leather clothes have been copied so many times down the generations that they are one of rock's visual cliches. His attitude has been borrowed in some part by most of rock's wannabe philosopher desperadoes and pretend warrior poets. His mike stand clutching stance has been aped by everyone from Patti Smith to Stiv Bators, to all those grunge geezers in lumberjack shirts, and even Julian Casablancas of the Strokes, although many probably don't even know it, and think they are copying Jim Morrison, Iggy Pop, or Johnny Rotten. When Jim Morrison asked Gene, 'How does it feel to be a major rock star?', it meant that, in comparison, and despite his own cultivated legend, Morrison felt essentially unworthy. But Gene was probably too drunk to answer.

Explaining Gene Vincent and why, thirty three years after his death, anyone should still be interested in the man, his music, and his radical rock 'n' roll image, is not easy, unless what, in the first chapter of this book, I call the 'oh-so primitive drama' of early rock 'n' roll is taken into account. To call Gene Vincent a totemic spirit is probably unduly mystical, but in rock – and in jazz and the blues before that – there have been always figures like Robert Johnson, Charlie Parker, Johnny Ace, Jim Morrison, Keith Moon, and Sid Vicious who were something over and above the music they created. Some were accepted as fundamental representations of the time and culture in which they lived and operated, and became the focus of what can only be described as modern tribal rituals, updated but still atavistic. They found themselves nominated as agents of a profound and ancient anarchy, that was still primally needed, even in the supposed sophistication of the twentieth and twenty-first centuries.

The coming of industrialization in Europe and America placed an impossible burden of conformity on western civilization. The population was expected to be factory friendly, and the old, somewhat chaotic peasant amusements were streamlined and standardized to fit the requirements of mass production. It hardly mattered whether the superstructure was capitalist or communist, the end result was stereotyped conformity; a lockstep adherence to narrow and oppressive norms. Sexual repression, and an overwhelming distrust of anyone who flaunted their individualism, or questioned the status quo in word, deed, or sound, became the order of the day. Hard work, mental health, monogamy, and sobriety were promoted as the only virtues, and they were instilled in schools, judicially enforced, and then reinforced by a cultural control that permitted no form of entertainment, be it book, film, or music, that was not considered 'good' for the mass audience. The safe standard for this kind of thought control was a mundane bloodlessness, in which sex was reduced to a snigger, and those who dissented were, at best, ghettoized in a small bohemian subworld that was only permitted to survive as long as it didn't do anything so overt that it bothered the population at large.

As late as 1960, a judge at the Old Bailey was asking a jury to consider whether DH Lawrence's *Lady Chatterley's Lover* was a book that they would permit their wives and

servants to read. Fortunately, at the same
time, The Beatles were singing 'Be-Bop-A-
Lula' in the sweaty darkness of Liverpool's
Cavern Club, while, in Moscow, Elvis Presley
records were being bootlegged, with the
grooves cut – one copy at a time – into used
X-ray plates. These underground, lo-fi
artifacts were known, with macabre Soviet
humour, as 'bone music'. The aftermath of
World War II had created the famous baby
boom, and a vast mass of young people were
taking a long look at what society had in
store for them and not liking it one bit. Post-
war youth was aware of the power of its own
sheer numbers, and, if any doubt remained, it
only had to look at the way the manu-
facturers of consumer products, and the
advertisers who worked from them
promoting those products were courting the
new spending power of the young. In the
mid-fifties, Hollywood, in its eager courtship
of this youth market, made a major mistake,
akin to selling guns to the Indians. Movie
producers sensed a feeling of rebellion in this
newly defined demographic of baby boom

teenagers, and used it as sales gimmick. James Dean, Marlon Brando, Steve McQueen and dozens of imitators were cast in movies and TV shows as the 'crazy mixed-up kid'. Although generally couched in terms of a salutary tale that any rebellion against what was good and wholesome would end badly, the kids of the time developed the ability to strip away the moral message, and groove on the cool of the moment. Okay, so the fictional juvenile delinquent on the screen would die at the end of the last act, death being infinitely preferable to going to jail, but before that final curtain, he had all the rule-breaking anti-establishment fun that the young audience craved.

In 1955, while Dean and Brando were at the peak of their teen popularity, Sam Phillips, in his small studio at Sun Records, had unwittingly compounded the problem. For a long time, Phillips had nursed the theory that, if he could find himself a handsome white boy who could sing R&B like a black blues shouter, he could make a fortune. Phillips, who had recorded artists like Howling Wolf and Rufus Thomas, knew that white kids in large numbers were tuning to black radio stations and buying records by black artists, looking for a more authentic energy and sexuality than could be found on the white end of the dial. Little Richard confirmed this with a bitter boast: 'The little white boys and girls had Pat Boone on the turntable, but my 45s were hidden in the drawer where their parents couldn't find them'.

Basic American racism had created one huge and vibrant pool of cultural potential that went totally unregulated as long as it stayed on it own Afro-American side of the tracks, and Phillips figured that, if he could find a white conduit to channel it into the mainstream, he would be made for life. What he didn't consider that it might also precipitate a radical cultural and political change that would fundamentally divert the course of history. When the Ku Klux Klan issued warnings to parents to stop their children from listening to 'nigger music' because it would undermine the position of the white race, they were spreading hate as usual, but they also saw more clearly than most, the changes that rock 'n' roll might bring about.

Sam Phillips found his boy in Elvis Presley, but sold out too early to make the fabulous fortune of his dreams. What happened instead was that he found himself part of the vast, and always expanding, fabulous legend that was rock 'n' roll. Phillips learned early that Elvis was too big for Sun Records. Indeed, Elvis was almost too big for rock 'n' roll, and certainly too big for himself. He was too good-looking, too talented, and his voice had too much of the x-factor that made women weak at the knees to be confined to any single role. He couldn't just be the white practitioner of rhythm and blues, or just the rock 'n' roll juvenile delinquent, the musical equivalent of James Dean. He may have started out as both, but Elvis generated too much money, and attracted too much pressure. After Ed Sullivan cut him off at the waist, he was doomed to be tamed. If Colonel Parker hadn't cut a deal to crop

Elvis' hair and march him off to the Army,
Elvis Presley probably would have been
assassinated much sooner than he actually
was, his power – before being diluted – was
that intense. But while Elvis was being made
into all things for all people, the highly
specific slot for the greasy bad boy of rock
became vacant, and that's how Gene Vincent
– whether he knew it or not – stepped up the
plate.

Gene had a magnificent voice, and a
awesome stage presence, but he neither had
the looks nor the frighteningly potent x-
factor of Elvis. What Gene had was what the
already quoted Simon Frith called 'tension'.
He sounded as though he was about to blow
a psychological fuse. He sound tightly
wrapped and dangerous. His records carried
the whiff of insanity, and his performances
were exercises in rock 'n' roll mayhem. In his
song 'Sweet Gene Vincent' Ian Dury wrote
the line, 'there's one in every town', meaning
that every community had it's quasi-romantic
outcast; the kid with the motorcycle; the
punk in the pool hall who has studied so

carefully exactly how to lean on his cue, and keep an unfiltered Pall Mall glued right of center to his lower lip; or the kid whose father drank and who the cops picked up after every outbreak of petty theft, or each time something got torched or vandalized; the kid with the girlfriend with too much lipstick who fell pregnant before her time. Gene Vincent became their personal representative in the rock pantheon, and was able to make them feel that he was singing his songs exclusively for them.

Gene was not only the original bad boy of rock, but he shaped the role so personally and exactly that all later aspirants had to pay him tribute and acknowledge his legacy. Of course, he had rivals, and other contenders could strike the pose, but none could surpass Gene as the real deal.

It would never have occurred to Gene Vincent to do anything but walk his agonizing and limping walk. In his blurred and intoxicated world of pain, he was incapable of doing otherwise, and he remained on what seemed to be his preordained outlaw course all the way to his grave beside the highway. That he should be fondly, even obsessively remembered so long after his death should not be a mystery. On the surface, it might appear that he left very little for future generations, a chaotic personal history of heavy drinking and four ruined marriages, a catalogue of intense recordings of simplistic songs that sound nursery-rhyme nonsensical when compared to the work of Lennon, Dylan, Townsend, Willie Nelson, or Jagger/Richards.

On paper, Jim Morrison seems quantum times the 'major rock star' that Gene ever was, and yet, in their respective deaths, the two men are nothing if not equal. Both have ugly headstones. The answer is that Gene Vincent set the template for a character without whom rock 'n' roll cannot exist with any real validity. Without the trash-romantic spirit of revolution, rock music can only be calculated, up-tempo dance music. In the final distillation, Gene Vincent's legacy to the world was a legend that had never been compromised.

That Europe should have been the place where his legend has been most assiduously preserved is another factor which, on the surface, defies easy explanation. The real answer is that rock meant something different in the USA and in Europe. In America, rock came easy. It was a disposable entertainment, readily available on TV and radio. It was used and all but thrown away, rarely considered, except by a few dedicated collectors as anything of more than transitory worth. In the UK, on the other hand, up until as late as 1966, rock music was severely curtailed by the BBC, and, in Gene's case, 'Woman Love' was banned outright. The situation was little better in France and Germany, and European rockers had to work a great deal harder for their music. When the virtual purge of rock 'n' roll took place in the US at the end of the fifties, Gene, Jerry Lee Lewis, and the rest of the original wild bunch were driven from the airwaves by congressional committees and the payola scandals, and replaced by Frankie Avalon and Bobby Rydell. Europe became the place of their exile, and, as such, treated these refugees with considerably more respect than they enjoyed in their homeland. The fans in Europe felt more of a sense of mission and dedication. For them, rock was history-in-the-making, and therefore had to be preserved at all cost.

Even today, Gene Vincent is still largely thought of in the USA as the man who recorded 'Be-Bop-A-Lula', but over the years, a niche has been carved for him as something more than a one-hit-wonder. The general transatlantic interplay of musical retrospective, and the fact that John Lennon, Dave Edmunds, and Jeff Beck have all recorded their Vincent tributes – in the case of Beck, an entire album of loving reproductions – have instigated a gradual rediscovery, and even brought Johnny Meeks and Cliff Gallup out of retirement to front Blue Caps revival bands. During the punk era in New York, Gene's portrait, in full leather regalia appeared on t-shirts and posters, and his image was increasingly used as the generic bad boy of yesterday. Perhaps more importantly, Hollywood has also rediscovered Gene, and songs of his have featured on movie soundtracks, usually as a piece of 1950's kitsch, but not always. In the magnificent 1990 Southern-gothic road-movie *Wild At Heart* (which critic Henry Cabot Beck called the 'Elvis film from Hell'), maverick director David Lynch used 'Be-Bop-A-Lula' as in important motif, along with a splendid '75 Cadillac El Dorado convertible, and a copy of Brando's snakeskin bike jacket from *The Fugitive Kind*. In *Wild At Heart*, Lynch made very clear that Gene Vincent was one of the high icons of demon kitsch.

Gene may be long gone, his life may not have been either happy or exemplary, and – as this biography attempts to show – the missed opportunities outweighed the triumphs. As Ian Dury so rightly told it, the chances really were slender and the beauties painfully brief. The strength of his legend may be more than the sum total of his recorded work, but his memory mercifully abides. And will abide for as long as rock itself continues. That, at least, is my profound hope. Bruce Springsteen may sing of 'no retreat, no surrender', but, without overtly stating it as such, that was the rule by which Gene Vincent both lived and died. I hope Gene is never forgotten because, apart from turning my own young life around, any future which denies him a place in the annals of rock 'n' roll will be a time when the music has become so pallid and meaningless it won't be worth a damn.

Epilogue

THE LONESOME DEATH OF GENE VINCENT

Oh mama, oh mama
This time I'm going down for sure
This time I'm going to hell
Like they always said I would

My ulcer's bleeding
And my bad leg's hurting
And the whiskey ain't helping
And the morphine don't make a dent
And outside this trailer
There's a world that I don't understand

They changed the rules, mama
They took the fins off the cars
And Jim Boy Morrison is wearing my old clothes
And it's 1971, Mama, not 1957
And Be-Bop-A-Lula's on welfare, mama
With two ugly kids and a bottle of 'ludes
Hustling truckers outside of Bakersfield
The dark cab of a White Freightliner
Ten bucks for a blowjob
And watch out for the gearshift baby
And you just watch out there, you hear

There's a smoke cloud rising, mama
And it's clouding up my head
Lucky Strike plain
In the old red and white pack
And the others are calling, mama
The ones who went before
Hank Williams is whispering
Hank says he wants to buy this kid a drink
And Eddie Cochran's got a new tune
That he wants to play me on his black guitar

I gotta go, mama
I gotta go soon

There's a woman waiting
With a red dress on
That old Whore of Babylon
Waiting to lay me down
That old Whore of Babylon
Wanting to take me down

I swear, mama
I swear before God
If I get through this
I'm going to be a better man
Kick is though, mama
I ain't gonna get through this
Kick is though, mama
Already I can feel the ulcer ripping
Kick is though, mama
Already I can taste the blood
I used to be a king, mama
I used to be a king
The Demon King
King of the fucking Jungle
And they kept me in a cage
I reminded them of too much
Said I was drunk on *American Bandstand*
Said I was a communist
Run out of the world by Dick Clark
And a bunch of assholes called Bobby

I used to have Cadillacs, mama
You ever hear of a communist with Cadillacs?
A caddy for every day of the week
And a white Corvette on sundays
But now
There's only one Cadillac left for me
And that's the long black rubber
Tired hearse, mama
that's the only Cadillac in my future
The graveyard's out by the freeway, mama
Out on some land that ought to be desert
If they didn't keep the sprinklers running
Twenty three hours a day
The graveyard's out by the freeway, mama
And the graveyard's hard to miss
Just take a left and follow the smell of diesel
All the way down the one one eight
And across the Ventura county line

Oh, mama, oh mama, you can't miss the
graveyard
You sure as shit can't miss the graveyard

Written 1992, first published 1995.

ACKNOWLEDGMENTS

All the Gene Vincent anecdotes that were told me down the years and especially those from the late Tony Secunda. Also Britt Hagarty's *The Day The Word Turned Blue* which supplied such a detailed factual framework, along with the very comprehensive liner notes from *Gene*, the EMI box set, by Steve Aynsley and Roger Nunn.

Mick Farren, Los Angeles, 2004

Gene Vincent: The Recording Sessions and Discography

COMPILED BY WAYNE 'DANG' DOOLEY

The information contained here is culled from various sources and is as accurate as it can be under the circumstances. Where information conflicts we accept the official record. The discography ignores low budget cash-ins and the countless 'best of' compilations put out since Gene's death.

The Recording
Sessions

Tracks are in order of recording and in session
taping sequence.

BLUE CAPS #1:

Musicans: Gene Vincent, vocals; Cliff Gallup, lead guitar; Dickie Harrell, drums and screams; Willie Williams, rhythm guitar; Jack Neal, upright bass. Recorded together until October 18th, 1956.

April 9th, 1956: WCMS studio, Nashville
Be-Bop-A-Lula (demo)/ Race With The Devil (demo)/ I Sure Miss You (demo)

May 4th, 1956: Owen Bradley's studio, Nashville.
Race With The Devil/ Be-Bop-A-Lula/ Woman Love/ I Sure Miss You.

May 24-27th, 1956, Owen Bradley's studio, Nashville.
Jezebel/ Crazy Legs/ Peg O'My Heart/ Wedding Bells /Waltz Of The Wind/ Ain't She Sweet/ Gonna Back Up, Baby/ Who Slapped John?/ Jumps Giggles And Shouts/ Bluejean Bop/ I Flipped/ Bop Street/ Well I Knocked (Bim

Bam)/ You Told A Fib/ Jump Back, Honey, Jump Back/

October 15th-18th, 1956, Owen Bradley's studio, Nashville.
Teenage Partner/ Blues Stay Away From Me/ Five Feet of Loving/ Cat Man/ Double Talking Baby/ Hold Me, Hug Me, Rock Me/ Unchained Melody/ B-I-Bickey-Bi, Bo-Bo-Go/ Pink Thunderbird/ Pretty Pretty Baby/ Cruisin'/ Important Words (1)/ You Better Believe/ Red Bluejeans And A Pony Tail/ Five Days, Five Days (with The Jordinaires).

BLUE CAPS #2

Musicians: Gene Vincent, vocals: Johnny Meeks, lead guitar; Dickie Harrell, drums; Bobby Jones, electric bass guitar; Paul Peek and Bubba Facenda, background vocals/hand clapping; Buck Owens played rhythm guitar; and on some songs The Jordanairies provided background vocals.

June 19th-20th, 1957, Hollywood Capitol Tower, LA.
I Got It/ Wear My Ring/ Lotta Lovin'/ Rollin' Danny/ Time Will Bring You Everything/ True To You/ In My Dreams/ Dance To The Bop.

December 6th, 9th-10th, 15th, 1957, Hollywood Capitol Tower, LA.
Your Cheatin' Heart/ Baby Blue/ Walkin' Home From School/ It's No Lie/ Should I Ever Love Again/ Flea Brain/ Brand New Beat/ Frankie & Johnnie/ You Belong To Me/ Keep It A Secret/ Yes, I Love You Baby/ By The Light Of The Silvery Moon/ Right Now/ You'll Never Walk Alone/ I Got A Baby

March 25th-29th, 1958, Hollywood Capitol Tower, LA. (Eddie Cochran sang backing vocals on some tracks)

Dance In The Street/ Git It/ I Love You/ Teenage Partner (2)/ Peace Of Mind/ Lovely Loretta/ Little Lover/ Rocky Road Blues/ Somebody Help Me/ Five Feet Of Lovin' (2)/ Look What You Gone And Done To Me/ Hey Good Looking/ Summertime/ I Can't Help It/ Wayward Wind/ Now Is The Hour

October 13th-16th, 19th-21st, 1958, Hollywood Capitol Tower, LA.

Lonesome Boy/ You Are The One For Me/ Maybe/ Got To Get To You Yet,/ My Heart/ The Night Is So Lonely/ Beautiful Brown Eyes/ Rip It Up/ Maybelline/ High Blood Pressure/ Say Mama/ Be Bop Boogie Boy/ I Can't Believe You Wanna Leave/ Who's Pushing Your Swing/ Anna Annabelle,/ Gone Gone Gone/ I Might Have Known,/ Important Words (2)/ My Baby Don't 'low,/ Over The Rainbow/ Ready Teddy/ Vincent's Blues. (This is the last appearance of Johnny Meeks until August 1969.)

August 3rd-6th, 1959, Hollywood Capitol Tower, LA.

Pretty Pearly/ Accentuate The Positive/ She She Little Sheila/ Darlene/ Why Don't You People Learn How To Drive/ Crazy Times/ Green Back Dollar/ Big Fat Saturday Night/ Wild Cat/ Hot Dollar/ Right Here On Earth/ Blue Eyes Cryin' In The Rain/ Everybody's Got A Date But Me/ Mitchiko From Tokyo.

The Blue Caps now disband and Gene Vincent travels to the UK.

AFTER THE BLUE CAPS

May 11th, 1960, Abbey Road Studios, London
Pistol Packin' Mama (with Georgie Fame and the Beat Boys)/ Weeping Willow (with the Norrie Paramor Orchestra).

January 10th-11th, 1961, Hollywood Capitol Tower, LA (with Jimmie Haskell Orchestra).
Crazy Beat/ I'm Gonna Catch Me A Rat/ It's Been Nice/ That's The Trouble With Love/ Good Lovin'/ Mister Loneliness/ Teardrops/ If You Want My Lovin'.

July 27th, Abbey Road Studios, London (with Sounds Incorporated)
I'm Going Home/ Love Of A Man.

October 18th, 1961, Hollywood Capitol Tower, LA (with Dave 'The Champs' Burgess Band)
Baby Don't Believe Him/ Lucky Star

November 30th, 1961, Abbey Road Studios, London (with Sounds Incorporated)
Spaceship To Mars/ There I Go Again.

July 3rd, 1962, London (produced by Bob Barratt)
King of Fools/ You're Still In My Heart/ Held For Questioning/ Be-Bop-A-Lula '62.

November 14th, 1963, London
Where Have You Been All My Life/ Temptation Baby/ The Beginning Of The End/ La Den Da Den Da Da/ Humpity, Dumpity/ A Love 'em And Leave Kinda Guy

March 16th, 1964, London
Love Love Love/ Lavender Blue/ You Are My Sunshine

May 15th, 1964, London
Slippin' And Slidin'/ Private Detective/ Shimmy Shammy Shingle/ Long Tall Sally/ Good Golly Miss Molly

May 23rd-24th, 1964, London
Send Me Some Lovin'/ Hey Hey Hey Hey/

Another Saturday Night/ Someday/ Baby Blue/
Susie Q

June 1966, Challenge, Hollywood, Ca.
Hurtin' For You Baby/ I'm A Lonesome
Fugitive/ Born To Be A Rolling Stone/ Hi Lili,
Hi Lo/ Poor Man's Prison/ Words And Music/
Bird Doggin'/ I've Got My Eyes On You/ Love
Is A Bird/ Ain't That Too Much/ Lonely Street/
Am I That Easy To Forget.

July 25th, 1967, Playground, Hollywood, Ca.
Story Of The Rockers/ Pickin' Poppies

*Mid-August, 1969 Los Angeles, USA (with
Johnny Meeks returning on lead guitar).*
Rockin' Robin/ In The Pines/ Be-Bop-A-Lula
'69/ Rainbow At Midnight/ Black Letter/ White
Lightning/ Sexy Ways/ Ruby Baby/ Lotta Lovin/
Circle Never Broken/ (I Heard That) Lonesome
Whistle/ Scarlet Ribbons (with Linda Ronstadt)

March 5th-8th, 1970, Hollywood Ca.
Sunshine/ I Need A Woman/ Slow Times
Comin'/ Danse Colinda/ Geese/ 500 Miles
Away From Home/ Listen To The Music/ If

Only You Could See Me Today/ A Million Shades Of Blue/ Tush Dog

October 17th, 20th, 1970, Hollywood, Ca.
How I Love Them Old Songs/ High On Life/ North Carolina Line/ You Can Make It If You Try/ There Is Something On Your Mind/ Our Souls/ The Day The World Turned Blue/ Boppin' The Blues/ Looking Back/ Oh Lonesome Me/ The Woman In Black

October 1st, 1971, London.
Say Mama /I'm Movin' On.

September 1971, Ron Weisner's apartment, Los Angeles.
Bring It On Home/ The Rose Of Love/ Hey Hey Hey Hey/ Party Doll

October 1st, 1971, London (with Richard Cole and the Kansas Hook band)
Say Mama/ Be-Bop-A-Lula/ Roll Over Beethoven/ Whole Lotta Shakin' (never released)/ Distant Drums (unrehearsed one-take cut).

DISCOGRAPHY
US Singles

1956

CAPITOL F 3450 Woman Love/ Be-Bop-A-Lula.

CAPITOL F 3530 Race With The Devil/ Gonna Back Up Baby.

CAPITOL F 3558 Bluejean Bop/ Who Slapped John?

1957

CAPITOL F 3617 Crazy Legs/ Important Words.

CAPITOL F 3678 Five Days, Five Days/ B-I-Bickey-Bi, Bo-Bo-Go.

CAPITOL F 3763 Wear My Ring/ Lotta Lovin', 1957.

CAPITOL F 3839 Dance To The Bop/ I Got It, 1957.

CAPITOL F 3871 Be-Bop-A-Lula/ Lotta Lovin' 1957.

1958

CAPITOL F 3874 I Got A Baby/ Walkin' Home from School.

CAPITOL F 3959 Baby Blue/ True to You.

CAPITOL F 4010 Rocky Road Blues/ Yes I Love You Baby.

CAPITOL F 4051 Git It/ Little Lover.

CAPITOL F 4105 Say Mama/ Be Bop Boogie Boy.

1959

CAPITOL F 4153 Over The Rainbow/ Who's Pushing Your Swing.

CAPITOL F 4237 Right Now/ The Night Is So Lonely. (The only US single to get a colour sleeve.)

CAPITOL F 4313 Wild Cat/ Right Here On

Earth. (Promotional copies with red label).

1960
CAPITOL F 4442 Anna Annabelle/ Pistol Packin' Mama.

1961
CAPITOL F 4525 If You Want My Lovin'/ Mister Loneliness.

1962
CAPITOL F 4665 Lucky Star/ Baby Don't Believe Him.

1966
CHALLENGE 59337 Bird Doggin'/ Ain't That Too Much.
CHALLENGE 59347 Lonely Street/ I've Got My Eyes on You.

1967
CHALLENGE 59365 Born To Be A Rolling Stone/ Hurtin' for You Baby.

1968
PLAYGROUND P-100 Story Of The Rockers/

Pickin' Poppies.

1969
FOREVER FR6001 Story Of The Rockers/ Pickin' Poppies. (Same tracks as previous release – a year later and a different label.)
ELEKTRA 74067 Be-Bop-A-Lula/ Lotta Lovin', 1969.

1970
KAMA SUTRA KA 514 Sunshine/ Geese.
KAMA SUTRA KA 518 The Day The World Turned Blue/ How I Love Them Old Songs.

1973
CAPITOL STARLINE 6042 Be-Bop-A-Lula/ Lotta Lovin'.

US EPs

1956

CAPITOL EAP 1-764 BLUEJEAN BOP, PART 1: Bluejean Bop/ Jezebel/ Ain't She Sweet/ Jumps Giggles And Shouts.

CAPITOL EAP 2-764 BLUEJEAN BOP, PART 2: Who Slapped John?/ Wedding Bells/ Up A Lazy River/ Bop Street.

CAPITOL EAP 3-764 BLUEJEAN BOP, PART 3: I Flipped/ Waltz Of The Wind/ Jump Back, Honey, Jump Back/ Peg O' My Heart.

1957

CAPITOL EAP 1-811 GENE VINCENT AND

THE BLUE CAPS, PART 1: Red Bluejeans And A Pony Tail/ Unchained Melody/ Hold Me, Hug Me, Rock Me/ You Told A Fib.

CAPITOL EAP 2-811 GENE VINCENT AND THE BLUE CAPS, PART 2: Cruisin'/ You Better Believe/ Double Talkin' Baby/ Blues Stay Away From Me.

CAPITOL EAP 3-811 GENE VINCENT AND THE BLUE CAPS, PART 3: Cat Man/ I Sure Miss You/ Pink Thunderbird/ Pretty Pretty Baby.

1958

CAPITOL EAP 1-970 GENE VINCENT ROCKS AND THE BLUE CAPS ROLL, PART 1: Frankie And Johnnie/ In My Dreams/ You'll Never Walk Alone/ Brand New Beat.

CAPITOL EAP 2-970 GENE VINCENT ROCKS AND THE BLUE CAPS ROLL, PART 2: By the Light Of The Silvery Moon/ Flea Brain/ Rollin' Danny/ Your Cheatin' Heart.

CAPITOL EAP 3-970 GENE VINCENT ROCKS AND THE BLUE CAPS ROLL, PART 3: You Belong To Me/ Time Will Bring You Everything/ Should I Ever Love Again/ It's No Lie.

CAPITOL EAP 1-985 HOT ROD GANG (from the movie): Dance In The Street/ Baby Blue/ Lovely Loretta/ Dance To The Bop.

CAPITOL EAP 1-1059 A GENE VINCENT RECORD DATE, PART 1: Five Feet Of Lovin'/ The Wayward Wind/ Somebody Help Me/ Keep It A Secret.

CAPITOL EAP 2-1059 A GENE VINCENT RECORD DATE, PART 2: Git It/ Teenage Partner/ Hey Good Lookin'/ I Can't Help It.

CAPITOL EAP 3-1059 A GENE VINCENT RECORD DATE, PART 3: Summertime/ I Love You/ Peace Of Mind/ Look What You Gone And Done To Me.

US & UK LPs:

1956

CAPITOL T764 BLUEJEAN BOP: Bluejean Bop/ Jezebel/ Ain't She Sweet/ Jumps Giggles And Shouts/ Who Slapped John?/ Wedding Bells/ Up A Lazy River/ Bop Street/ I Flipped/ Waltz Of The Wind/ Jump Back, Honey, Jump Back/ Peg O' My Heart.

1957

CAPITOL T811 GENE VINCENT AND THE BLUE CAPS: Red Bluejeans And A Pony Tail/ Unchained Melody/ Hold Me, Hug Me, Rock

Me/ You Told A Fib/ Cruisin'/ You Better Believe/ Double Talkin' Baby/ Blues Stay Away From Me/ Cat Man/ I Sure Miss You/ Pink Thunderbird/ Pretty Pretty Baby.

CAPITOL T970 GENE VINCENT ROCKS AND THE BLUE CAPS ROLL: Frankie And Johnnie/ In My Dreams/ You'll Never Walk Alone/ Brand New Beat/ By the Light Of The Silvery Moon/ Flea Brain/ Rollin' Danny/ Your Cheatin' Heart/ You Belong To Me/ Time Will Bring You Everything/ Should I Ever Love Again/ It's No Lie.

1958

CAPITOL T1009 TEENAGE ROCK 1958 (on an LP with Ferlin Husky, Sonny James and Tommy Sands) Gene's songs: Dance To The Bop/ Be-Bop-A-Lula/ Lotta Lovin'/ Well I Knocked (Bim Bam).

CAPITOL T1059 A GENE VINCENT RECORD DATE: Five Feet Of Lovin'/ The Wayward Wind/ Somebody Help Me/ Keep It A Secret/ Hey Good Lookin'/ Git It/ Teenage Partner/ Peace Of Mind/ Look What You Gone And Done To Me/ Summertime/ I Can't Help It/ I Love You.

1959
CAPITOL T1207 SOUNDS LIKE GENE VINCENT: My Baby Don't 'low/ I Can't Believe You Want To Leave/ I Might Have Known/ In Love Again/ You Are The One For Me/ Ready Teddy/ I Got to Get to You Yet/ Vincent's Blues/ Maybe Now Is The Hour/ My Heart/ Maybelline.

1960
CAPITOL T1342 & ST1342 CRAZY TIMES: Crazy Times/ She She Little Sheila/ Darlene/ Everybody's Got A Date But Me/ Why Don't You People Learn How To Drive/ Green Back Dollar/ Big Fat Saturday Night/ Mitchiko from Tokyo/ Hot Dollar/ Accentuate The Positive/ Blue Eyes Cryin' In The Rain/ Pretty Pearly.

1963
CAPITOL T20453 (UK) THE CRAZY BEAT OF GENE VINCENT: Crazy Beat/ Important Words/ It's Been Nice/ Lonesome Boy/ Good Lovin'/ I'm Gonna Catch Me A Rat/ Rip It Up/ High Blood Pressure/ That's The Trouble With Love/ Weeping Willow/ Teardrops/ Gone Gone Gone.

1964

COLUMBIA 33 SX1646 (UK) SHAKIN' UP A STORM: Hey Hey Hey Hey/ Lavender Blue/ Private Detective/ Shimmy Shammy Shingle/ Someday/ Another Saturday Night/ Slippin' And Slidin'/ Long Tall Sally/ Send Me Some Lovin'/ Love Love Love/ Good Golly Miss Molly/ Baby Blue/ Susie Q/ You Are My Sunshine.

1967

LONDON HAH8333 (UK) GENE VINCENT: Hurtin' For You Baby/ I'm A Lonesome Fugitive/ Born To Be A Rolling Stone/ Hi Lili, Hi Lo/ Poor Man's Prison/ Words And Music/ Bird Doggin'/ I've Got My Eyes On You/ Love Is A Bird/ Ain't That Too Much/ Lonely Street/ Am I That Easy To Forget.

1969

DANDELION D9 102 I'M BACK AND I'M PROUD: Rockin' Robin/ In The Pines/ Be-Bop-A-Lula '69/ Rainbow At Midnight/ Black Letter/ White Lightning/ Sexy Ways/ Ruby Baby/ Lotta Lovin '69/ Circle Never Broken/ I Heard That Lonesome Whistle/ Scarlet Ribbons

CAPITOL DKAO 380 GENE VINCENT'S GREATEST HITS: Be-Bop-A-Lula/ Little Lover/ Race With The Devil/ Important Words ('58)/ She She Little Sheila/ Bluejean Bop/ Woman Love/ Maybelline/ Over The Rainbow/ Lotta Lovin'/ Yes I Love You Baby.

1970
KAMA SUTRA KSBS2019 IF ONLY YOU COULD SEE ME TODAY: Sunshine/ I Need A Woman to Love/ Slow Times Comin'/ Danse Colinda/ Geese/ 500 Miles Away From Home/ Listen To The Music/ If Only You Could See Me Today/ A Million Shades Of Blue/ Tush Dog.

1971
KAMA SUTRA KSBS2027 THE DAY THE WORLD TURNED BLUE: How I Love Them Old Songs/ High On Life/ North Carolina Line/ You Can Make It If You Try/ Our Souls/ There Is Something On Your Mind/ The Day The World Turned Blue/ Boppin' The Blues/ Looking Back/ Oh Lonesome Me/ The Woman In Black.

1974

CAPITOL ST11287 THE BOP THAT WON'T STOP: (Two previously unreleased songs on this greatest hits album... Teenage Partner and Five Feet Of Lovin'... both originally recorded in 1956). Bop Street intro/ Be-Bop-A-Lula/ Race With The Devil/ The Devil/ Woman Love/ I Sure Miss You/ Crazy Legs/ Who Slapped John?/ Bluejean Bop/ Teenage Partner '56/ Five Feet Of Lovin' '56/ Cruisin'/ Important Words/ B-I-Bickey-Bi, Bo-Bo-Go/ Bop Street outro.

1979

CAPITOL SM 380 GENE VINCENT'S GREATEST HITS: Be-Bop-A-Lula/ Little Lover/ Race With The Devil/ Important Words ('58)/ She She Little Sheila/ Bluejean Bop/ Woman Love/ Maybelline/ Lotta Lovin'/ Yes I Love You Baby.

1980

ROLLIN ROCK LP022 FOREVER GENE VINCENT: Bring It On Home/ The Rose Of Love/ Hey Hey Hey Hey/ Party Doll/ Plus various songs by Gene's daughter, Johnny Meeks, Johnny Carroll, Ray Campi and others.

1987

STRANGE FRUIT DEI 80001-2 (CD) THE LAST SESSION: Say Mama/ Be-Bop-A-Lula/ Roll Over Beethoven/ Distant Drums.

1990

CAPITOL/EMI CDS 7 94592 2 THE GENE VINCENT 6-CD BOX SET: 151 Capitol and Columbia masters, 29 previously unreleased out-takes and a 48-page booklet including rare photographs.

CD1: Race With The Devil/ Be-Bop-A-Lula/ Woman Love/ I Sure Miss You/ Jezebel/ Crazy Legs/ Peg O'My Heart/ Wedding Bells (Are Breaking Up That Old Gang Of Mine)/ Waltz Of The Wind/ Up A Lazy River/ Ain't She Sweet/ Gonna Back Up Baby/ Who Slapped John?/ Jumps Giggles And Shouts/ Blue Jean Bop/ I Flipped/ Bop Street/ Well I Knocked (Bam Bam)/ You Told A Fib/ Jump Back/ Honey/ Teenage Partner/ Blues Stay Away From Me/ Five Feet Of Lovin'/ Catman/ Double Talkin' Baby/ Hold Me Hug Me Rock Me/ Unchained Melody/ B-I-Bickey-Bi, Bo-Bo-Go

CD2: Pink Thunderbird/ Pretty Pretty Baby/ Cruisin'/ Important Words/ You Better Believe/

Red Blue Jeans And A Ponytail/ Five Days, Five Days/ I Got It/ Wear My Ring/ Lotta Lovin'/ Rollin' Danny/ Time Will Bring You Everything/ True To You/ In My Dreams/ Dance To The Bop/ Your Cheatin' Heart/ Baby Blue/ Walkin' Home From School/ It's No Lie/ Should I Ever Love Again/ Flea Brain/ Brand New Beat/ Frankie And Johnnie/ You Belong To Me/ Keep It A Secret/ Yes I Love You Baby/ By The Light Of The Silvery Moon/ Right Now/ You'll Never Walk Alone

CD3: I Got It Baby/ Dance In The Street/ Git It I Love You/ Teenage Partner/ Peace Of Mind/ Lovely Loretta/ Little Lover/ Rocky Road Blues/ Somebody Help Me/ Five Feet Of Lovin'/ Look What You've Gone And Done To Me/ Hey Good Lookin'/ Summertime/ I Can't Help It (If I'm Still In Love With You)/ The Wayward Wind/ Now Is The Hour/ Lonesome Boy/ You Are The One For Me/ Maybe/ I've Got To Get You Yet/ My Heart/ The Night Is So Lonely/ Beautiful Brown Eyes/ Rip It Up

CD4: Maybellene/ High Blood Pressure/ In Love Again/ Say Mama/ Be Bop Boogie Boy/ I Can't Believe You Wanna Leave/ Who's Pushin' Your Swing/ Anna-Annabelle/ Gone Gone

Gone/ I Might Have Known/ Important Words/ My Baby Don't 'Low/ Over The Rainbow/ Ready Teddy/ Vincent's Blues/ Pretty Pearly/ Accentuate The Positive/ She She Little Sheila/ Darlene/ Why Don't You People Learn How To Drive?/ Crazy Times/ Greenback Dollar/ Big Fat Saturday Night

CD5: Wild Cat/ Hot Dollar/ Right Here On Earth/ Blue Eyes Cryin' In The Rain/ Everybody's Got A Date But Me/ Mitchiko From Tokyo/ Pistol Packin' Mama/ Weeping Willow/ Crazy Beat/ I'm Gonna Catch Me A Rat/ It's Been Nice (Goodnight)/ That's The Trouble With Love/ Good Lovin'/ Mister Loneliness/ Teardrops/ If You Want My Lovin'/ Spaceship To Mars/ There I Go Again (Whoops I'm Dreaming)/ I'm Going Home (To See My Baby)/ Love Of A Man

CD6: Baby Don't Believe Him/ Lucky Star/ The King Of Fools/ You're Still In My Heart/ Held For Questioning/ Be-Bop-A-Lula/ Where Have You Been All My Life/ Temptation Baby/ The Beginning Of The End/ La Den Da Den Da Da/ Humpity Dumpity/ ALove 'Em And Leave 'Em Kinda Guy/ Love Love Love/ Lavender Blue/ You Are My Sunshine/ Slippin' And Slidin'/

Private Detective/ Shimmy Shammy Shingle/ Long Tall Sally/ Good Golly Miss Molly/ Send Me Some Lovin'/ Hey Hey Hey Hey/ Another Saturday Night/ Someday (You'll Want Me To Want You)/ Baby Blue/ Susie Q

2004

EMI 5957672 (UK) DANCE TO THE BOP: Race With The Devil/ Well I Knocked (And I Knocked)/ Crazy Legs/ Important Words/ Cruisin'/ Be-Bop-A-Lula/ Who Slapped John?/ Unchained Melody/ Red Blue Jeans And A Ponytail/ Woman Love/ Pink Thunderbird/ I Sure Miss You/ Teenage Partner/ Bluejean Bop/ I Got A Baby/ Lotta Lovin'/ In My Dreams/ Yes I Love You Baby/ Baby Blue/ Dance To The Bop/ You'll Never Walk Alone/ Git It/ Rocky Road Blues/ Say Mama/ Beautiful Brown Eyes/ My Heart/ Over The Rainbow/ Wild Cat/ She She Little Sheila/ Pistol Packin' Mama

The Do-Not Press
Fiercely Independent Publishing

Keep in touch with what's happening at the
cutting edge of independent British
publishing.

Simply send your name and address to:
The Do-Not Press (gene)
16 The Woodlands, London SE13 6TY (UK)

or email us: gene@thedonotpress.com

There is no obligation to purchase
(although we'd certainly like you to!)
and no salesman will call.

___

Visit our regularly-updated website:

www.thedonotpress.com
Mail Order

All our titles are available from good bookshops, or
(in case of difficulty) direct from The Do-Not Press
at the address above. There is no charge for post
and packing for orders to the UK and Europe.

(NB: A post-person may call.)